Understanding Wisdom

A Treatise on Wisdom Viewed from the Second Cognition

By

Endall Beall

First Edition

Dedication

This book is dedicated to humanity, which has great potential as a species, as yet to be realized.

Table of Contents

ACKNOWLEDGEMENTS

I would like to acknowledge the wisdom teachers of the past who have left humanity the genuine wisdom to advance itself as a species – Siddhartha Guatama (Buddha), Jesus of Nazareth (Immanuel), Friedrich Nietzsche and Don Juan Matús.

INTRODUCTION

Throughout time and recorded written human history philosophers and intellectuals have pondered and argued over what constitutes wisdom. Even when one looks up the definition of wisdom and its synonyms in the dictionary, they can come away scratching their head trying to understand what wisdom actually is. Wisdom is defined as:

1.   the quality of having experience, knowledge, and good judgment; the quality of being wise

2.   the soundness of an action or decision with regard to the application of experience, knowledge, and good judgment.

3.   the body of knowledge and principles that develops within a specified society or period.

If we look at our world today, using the first two definitions, we do not find much wisdom in use by humanity where we spend vast sums of money creating nuclear power plants that create radioactive spent fuel rods with radioactivity that will last tens of thousands of years, which we have no clue how to neutralize for the safety of ourselves and future generations. We also see no wisdom, and surely no common sense, when we spend more money on weapons of war and means to destroy ourselves while our cities and road systems fall into disrepair and people go hungry, unable to find jobs to support themselves.

There is no wisdom, and surely no common sense with a species which is controlled by a handful of elite, self-appointed and unelected bureaucratic overlords who secretly control our governments from behind the scenes while the public is blissfully and willfully ignorant to their machinations. Nor do we find any wisdom or common sense when the corporations owned and controlled by these elite are involved in genetically manipulating the seed stock of humanity's food crops to make our food supply non-regenerative and able to only grow one crop, thereby destroying nature's ability to grow regenerative food plants, all for the sake of creating a monopolistic dependency on these corporations for our very food. Yet it is these elite who consider themselves the wise men and intellectuals of our era, hiding their tyranny behind the mask of 'scientific advancement'.

The third definition above refers to what is generally known as 'conventional wisdom', which is defined as "a generally accepted theory or belief". Theories are unproven tenets, meaning that they are ideas based on conjecture and often supported by 'reason', the watchword and God of these elite controllers ever since the so-called Age of Enlightenment or Age of Reason. Beliefs, on the other hand, are even more tenuous than theories because they are based on something that a person hopes and wishes was true. A truly wise individual would recognize that theories and beliefs are not very strong foundations through which to interpret and define reality, but if one is only dealing with superficial cognitive perceptions based on theories and beliefs, then neither wisdom nor common sense are going to be found in much abundance. It is the perception and the illusion of beliefs that runs the world, and we see genuine wisdom exhibited in very few individuals indeed.

Conventional wisdom is nothing more than a commonly held belief system within any given culture, and it changes through time, so it is therefore not real wisdom, but is in fact consensus agreement based on public perceptions. The handful of elite controllers know that if one can manipulate public perceptions, they can create a semblance of reality, a simulacrum of reality based on illusion and false perceptions. This is how humanity is presently controlled worldwide. Through manipulation of the media, the educational systems, religions and political systems worldwide, this handful of self-appointed, elite controllers keep this cognitive illusion of reality alive, ensuring that humanity remains cognitively enslaved and possessing very little true wisdom. This is how conventional wisdom is created, through consensus beliefs in what we are told by others, and very seldom through any actual experience of our own. Humanity lives in a second-hand reality, living its life through traditions handed down by one god or another, through priesthoods and political systems devised by others, and always subject to the semblance of authority by those who are shrewd enough to foist their own beliefs onto you by claiming either their intellectual or spiritual superiority.

There are two primary definitions for the word shrewd. The first is *"marked by clever discerning awareness and hardheaded acumen - shrewd common sense."* The second definition, unfortunately, is how the word shrewd is applicable in more modern perceptions, and that is, *"given to wily and artful ways or dealing - a shrewd operator."* Few people use genuine common sense any more, for presumed common sense is governed by controlled perceptions dictated to us by very wily, deceitful and shrewd elitists who define how common sense should be measured according to their own agenda. These controllers may think they are wise, but in fact they are very shrewd deceivers, hiding behind the curtains of consensus perceptions, which they naturally control to their own advantage over the rest of humanity.

A true person of wisdom can see past the illusion of consensus reality, can see through conventional wisdom, to see the reality behind the cognitive scam. A true person of wisdom can not only see the errors of humanity's ways, but is wise enough to call those errors to the attention of humanity. Unfortunately, the true sage is most often misunderstood and misinterpreted in the world of conventional wisdom and consensus reality, and is usually vilified for pointing out the truths that the masses simply do not want to hear, much less do anything to change for the better.

This short volume is a treatise on wisdom that will hopefully settle the matter of what real wisdom is and finally put to rest the confusion that the majority of philosophers throughout time have not figured out.

1. What is Wisdom?

For us to understand wisdom beyond how it is presently understood, we will have to take a look at a wise man or two in order to establish a standard of measurement. One of the earliest known wise men, or sages, was the Chinese philosopher Lao Tze or Lao Tzu. For a number of years, I heard people talk about the wisdom of Lao Tzu and how his wisdom teachings were hard for many people to grasp. With this information in hand, I first approached his work, the *Tao Te Ching*, expecting to find the typical Eastern philosophical riddles loaded with mystical overtones. Instead, what I found was a book filled with common sense teachings that I had no problem grasping at all. I really couldn't understand why people had such a hard time comprehending his commonsense teachings.

General scholarly assessment places the composition of the *Tao Te Ching* in the 6th century BC, and it predated the teachings of Buddha, another accepted wise man, by about a century. The *Tao Te Ching* can be translated to mean either, "The Classic of the Way's Virtues," or "The Book of the Way of Virtue." When we look into these ancient wisdom traditions and the originators of them, we always find the historicity of these sages in question. The lack of historical evidence of their existence is present with not only Lao Tzu, but with Siddhartha

Guatama (the Buddha), and the man they called Jesus in the Bible. In the teachings of all three of these historically questionable individuals we find core truths that humanity in general still does not fully comprehend because it lacks the cognitive wherewithal to understand them when compared to their conventional wisdom and its first cognition consensus reality.

In my book *Willful Evolution,* I provided explanations about the principles of two separate systems of cognitive awareness. Virtually all of humanity operates under a cognitive system I call the first cognition, and I call it that because every human being starts from, and is indoctrinated into, that system of consciousness. To advance into a higher state of cognitive awareness, what I call the second cognition, requires transcending the first cognition system of awareness in order for the individual to see the world with new eyes and broader perceptions.

When the Yaqui shaman Don Juan Matús tried to teach Carlos Castenada his system of wisdom, he stated categorically that the world of what he called the spirit warrior, or sorcerer, taught that there are two separate and distinct forms of consciousness. Castenada totally misunderstood those teachings and turned the teachings into mystical adventures with himself playing the star of the show, and the teachings got overshadowed with mystical nonsense advocating hallucinogenic drug use to attain enlightenment. Like his forerunners who tried to explain advanced cognitive awareness, the existence of anyone called don Juan is also thrown into question and many critics of Carlos Castenada feel that he was only a fictional character borne from Castenada's vivid imagination.

7

Buddha coined his own term to describe this alternate form of consciousness and called it Nirvana, where don Juan called it the sorcerer's way. Lao Tzu called it 'The Way', and the man they called Jesus referred to this expanded level of cognitive awareness as being 'born again'. Each of these teachers taught that growth into this different form of cognitive awareness was an individual endeavor, just as I did when I presented *Willful Evolution*. Every one of these teachers subsequently had their teachings corrupted by people living in the first cognition system of awareness who insisted that the teachings fit into their own limited cognitive perceptual boxes of understanding, thereby leading to cult followings that in many cases turned into institutionalized, mystical religions. These are specific examples of what happens to real wisdom when it is provided to those who have no understanding of that wisdom. This is exactly why Jesus warned to not cast pearls (of wisdom) before swine. These pearls will always be misinterpreted and corrupted by ignorant people operating in the first cognition consensus perceptual reality. It has happened time and again throughout the ages, and the wisdom they taught is still mysterious and misunderstood by humanity at large.

In more ancient times wisdom was usually associated with the goddess; the Mother Goddess, the Virgin Goddess, or a combination of both in most cases. In ancient Greece, this goddess was Athena, whose symbol was the owl. In Rome, she was known as Minerva, or Pallas Athena, who was also symbolized by the owl, which is where we get the modern ideas about the wise old owl. In ancient Sumeria, the owl was the symbol of the goddess

Inanna, also referred to as *nin-ninna*, or Divine Lady of the Owl. The wisdom of the ancient Triple Goddess has since been bestowed on the mother of Jesus, Mary, who is known in the Catholic Church as "The Seat of All Wisdom." This tradition of ancient goddess wisdom keeps being repackaged for new audiences who have no understanding about where the traditions originated.

In the East, in Indian Hindu traditions, the goddess of wisdom is Saraswati, one part of the 'triple goddess' with Lakshmi and Parvati. The goddess traditions and their association with the arts, writing and wisdom are ancient indeed. I explained the nature of the goddess cults in my book, *We Are Not Alone – Part 3: The Luciferian Agenda of the Mother Goddess.*

The goddess tradition, utilizing the owl as its symbol, can be found in the symbols of the Illuminati, formed in 1776 by Adam Weishaupt, who was raised in Jesuit school, and who some claim was a Jesuit himself. The owl symbol is also found at the Bohemian Grove where a 40-foot statue of an owl is used in pagan rituals by some of the most powerful men on the planet every July. Bohemian Grove is located at Monte Rio, California and its existence and attendees cannot be effectively refuted.

The owl holds different interpretations to many different people worldwide. In many Native American traditions, seeing an owl is considered a harbinger of death, and this same belief can be found in ancient Mayan beliefs. Others profess that the owl can see in the dark, and that this ability allows the owl to see through deception and trickery, where the dark signifies the world of perceptual illusion. Within similar traditions, the death associated with the owl is not a physical death, but the death of a certain form of consciousness that can lead to enlightenment and wisdom. It is this death of one system of consciousness into another greater sense of consciousness that Jesus referred to with the term 'born again'.

In the first cognition world, where human consciousness presently functions, true wisdom has been bastardized and corrupted into conventional wisdom where we accredit people with being 'streetwise', being clever and deceptive, or somehow more intellectually advanced, as in the case of academics, philosophers, and religious gurus. Attaining true wisdom has less to do with intellectual pursuits and philosophy than it does with advancing one's perceptual capabilities to see clearly through the illusion of the first cognition perceptual world and its consensus realities. This is what philosophers throughout time have not understood, and this explains why pure intellectualism and reason on their own will not lead one to second cognition awareness.

Within the consensus realities around the world, people's perceptions are shaped by their local and national cultures. The consensus reality of India is not the same as the consensus reality found in the Philippines, Australia, Europe and the United States. Although we find the European Union, contrived by the same Marxist-oriented elite controlled by the Fabian Society, every European nation within the EU has its own consensus reality differing between the Latins, the French, the British, the Germans, etc. Each of these varied consensus realities are governed and controlled by ancient traditions which every people around the planet hangs onto as part of their personal ego identity, and each of these consensus realities has its own form of conventional wisdom, once again illustrating that conventional wisdom is not wisdom at all, but merely a perception of wisdom within specific human cultural herds.

Cultural traditions were generally established by the beliefs in ancient gods and their mandates on mankind. Although modern atheistic scholarship would rather discount the idea that these ancient gods actually existed and are only the stuff of myth, the God syndrome has poisoned the psyche of humanity around the planet for thousands of years. This God syndrome is what spawned the rise of Atheism, for without the God syndrome Atheism would have no purpose to exist as an ideology. In essence, Atheism has become the religion of the non-religious, worshipping its god Reason, and using that as the justification to discount everything except science and intellectualism as the pinnacles of human capabilities.

Within the ranks of these Fabian elite we find those who believe that the human race on this planet is of faulty design, so for more than a century now they have been working to modify the human being into their own twisted version of evolution through what is called Transhumanism. Their ideas on the 'improvement' of humanity have resulted in the practice of Eugenics, i.e. selective breeding; gene splicing animal and human genetics seeking to 'improve' the human model into a type of *Island of Dr. Moreau* nightmare; or through 'perfecting' humanity by merging humans and machines into any number of varied cyborg hybrids. H.G. Wells, the author of *The Island of Dr. Moreau*, was an early Fabian Society member and many of his writings push forth the Fabian ideologies, both in his fiction and non-fiction books.

With everything just presented we find very little wisdom. We find humanity controlled by traditions handed down by elitist gods, elitist priests, elitist kings and dictatorial emperors, and in our era, elitist unelected armies of Fabian Marxist bureaucrats controlling governments around the globe behind the scenes worldwide. Under these systems of strict authoritarian control, humanity has never made a decision about shaping its own future or destiny as a species. Everything we believe and perceive has been handed down to us by authorities throughout the ages, and humanity willingly buys into these authoritarian ideologies generation after generation because 'it is tradition'. It seems that few average individuals question these traditions once they have been accepted, and most people actually serve as vicious guardians of these traditions out of fear that breaking tradition just might bring down the wrath of God upon them, that their culture might collapse, or that their government might put them in jail for not walking in lockstep with the consensus reality.

Humanity is cognitively lazy. The human psyche is controlled by the authority syndrome at every turn, and this occurs because humans have bought into the cognitive lie that the cream rises to the top and only the best and smartest are qualified to lead the rest of the human herd. Yet in our modern world, more and more people are seeing that what rises to the top of the human herds are elitists who hold themselves above the laws they pass for others to follow, and corruption is no longer the exception but the rule. Even in the face of this realization, no one wants to break from this authoritarian tradition, choosing instead to follow along and bitch about what they see and doing nothing to change themselves to escape the cognitive tyranny that holds their consciousness captive. There is neither wisdom nor common sense to be found when we view this harsh truth about humanity.

It is much easier to deny the existence of an authoritarian conspiracy of the magnitude perpetrated by little-known organizations like the Fabian Society, which was created in Great Britain in 1884, than it is to think that corruption and authoritarian control lies only in the hands of individuals who can be corrupted. The mind of the average person in the streets is one of blissful ignorance and living a perceptual illusion. Their personal affairs and comfort are generally all they are interested in, and not that many will move beyond their cognitive comfort zones of perceived reality to face the truth. Their consensus perception of reality and their conventional wisdom is all that most feel they need to navigate through life until they get the dirt blanket at the end of their lives.

For many, the only joy in their lives is found through escapist endeavors – retreats to Disneyland, drug and alcohol use, staying glued to a TV set in their off-work hours, or living lives of fantasy lost in video game addictions or watching sports. In the poorer parts of the world people spend their time just trying to survive and get a day's worth of food and water into their bellies to get them through their miserable lives, all so they can repeat the same life of desperation the next day. The fact is that humanity doesn't care about humanity, it only cares about satisfying its own individual needs and little else. Although the Fabian elitists use their propaganda machines to tout humanitarianism, it is nothing but a false front to hide a much darker agenda of controlling the masses through cognitive mind control and the manipulation of perceptions of a false reality. This is true in every nation around the planet and the only exceptions are those to be found in isolated tribal villages far removed from the influences of this technological nightmare, but even these remote tribes are still controlled by the beliefs in their gods and their authoritarian headmen or shamans. No one escapes these systems.

2. Human Nature – Really?

Everywhere we turn in the field of Psychology we hear the term 'human nature' used without end. We use the term ourselves and we believe that we have some understanding about human nature, but is it *really* human nature, or is it simply the habits of traditions and beliefs foisted on us by authoritarian figures throughout the ages that have programmed these behaviors we assume are human nature? Are we really the person we think we are, or are we simply the product of cultural programming that convinces us of the illusion of our very personalities?

Within the fields of science and psychology the argument over whether we are shaped by the nature of our genetics, or by the environment and cultural milieu in which we are raised is still a major point of contention. This is the 'nature versus nurture' argument, and it remains unsettled, with advocates on both sides of the divide actively defending their positions. These experts fall prey to their ideas about what comprises human nature and they use present human behavior as their measuring stick, exhibiting no wisdom to perceive that maybe human nature is more than how humanity has been programmed through multiple generations of traditions and beliefs. They observe how humans act and take the evidence presented at face value, never perceiving that perhaps there is something more to the human equation than social compliance through which to perceive human consciousness.

Standards of 'normalcy' are measured against the society in general, and one who complies with the laws, doesn't make waves and can navigate through life without emotional disruption is considered normal when compared to the rest of the culture. When one falls into challenging cultural norms, or can't deal with the emotional pressure of their native culture, is when the psychologist or psychiatrist enters the picture to attempt to repair this disrupted ego and make it fit back into its cultural herd. For all intents and purposes, the head doctors are simply ego repairmen, working to help the individual ego cope with its emotional anxieties and fit back into a position of normality within their cultural mandates.

Gustave Le Bon posited the theory of Crowd Psychology, and many of his observations on the matter were very astute regarding the psyche of the masses. Unfortunately, his theory has been expanded upon by the elite authoritarian Fabian controllers of this planet and has been turned into a weapon of mass psychological control. Humanity at large has no working concept about how they are having their consciousness and perceptions manipulated in this manner, and if you tell most people about it, they utterly refuse to believe that they can be manipulated so easily. Everything they believe has been fed to them by authority figures who most of humanity accepts as the wisest and most intelligent of our species, but such is not the case.

What the keen observer notes is that it is the psychopathic personality that gravitates to positions of power and authority, with sociopaths playing secondary roles in the bureaucracies that are growing in leaps and bounds around the planet. Dmitri Orlov made this same observation, with which I wholeheartedly agree, in his book *Shrinking the Technosphere*. When we have cultures that nurture and feed conscienceless psychopaths and let them rise to positions of power, we see a species that exhibits little to no wisdom at all. Refusal to admit such observations when they are provided, whether out of denial, or protecting one's cultural belief system, borders on the insane, again exhibiting no wisdom or common sense. But within the realm of first cognition consciousness, this is the norm, not the exception.

Humanity lives within a closed loop system of continually reinforced beliefs in propaganda of all kinds; cultural, religious, commercial and political. Every perception humanity embraces, not only as their reality, but what shapes their very consciousness, is designed by others and fed to the masses by others, and the masses believe that their actions and behaviors are their own. Even the minds of the practitioners of psychology and psychiatry are controlled by the same propagandized cultural indoctrination and institutional learning that shaped their professions, and which enforces its own rules by peer compliance to walk in lockstep together. To challenge the status quo is the death knell to one's career in this field or any other academically controlled environment on the planet. Don't buck the system or you are going to pay for it. Unfortunately, this is exactly how humanity, as a whole, polices itself and keeps it consciousness in chains, all the while believing it is preserving something of value. The only thing truly being preserved is cognitive mediocrity and repetitive, multi-generational brainwashing to preserve the cultural status quo.

Our environment shapes our consciousness. Starting with our parenting, we are first indoctrinated with their beliefs which they insist they must pass on to their children. In the majority of cases our religious beliefs were instilled in us at a very young age based on our parents trying to replicate themselves through their children into Hindus. Muslims, Buddhists or Christians. The child has no choice in these settings of familial indoctrination and multi-generational brainwashing for, in truth, that is what it is. The wise individual can see this repeating cycle of brainwashing and develops the wisdom to step away from such indoctrination.

Aside from parental indoctrination, children continue this indoctrinated programming through watching television and being introduced to more stringent cultural programming when they step into the educational system. The Fabian Society has been very successful in taking over the educational system and turning schools into indoctrination mills designed to create more cogs in their socialist belief machine of Liberal-Capitalism. They dictate the acceptable curriculum and set the standards for who gets elevated within this system for toeing the line and striving to be the best of the indoctrinated. This system rewards itself, not the individual. The individual that bucks the system, the child who doesn't fall into step with the educational party line, is ostracized, failed, disciplined or ***drugged*** into compliance. This is how our children are turned into cognitive robots and nothing more than acceptable members of the cultural herd. Wash, rinse, repeat. This is how the public schools have been manipulated for over a century under the watchful eye of the Fabian Society and its wealthy associates like the Rockefeller and Ford Foundations.

Through ownership and control of mass media, the corporate giants manage and dictate the images and stories they sell to the public to keep the consensus perception in place. Through media manipulation and the abuse of crowd psychology, nations and cultures can either be unified or divided as it suits the Fabian agenda for total global control and their fantasized world government. Control the perceptions of the masses and you can make nations rise into a war frenzy or collapse through creating internal dissent between a nation's people. The power and use of propaganda is not a new invention, but in this current technological era, the technique has become highly refined when coupled with crowd psychology, and it has been devastatingly effective to control global cultures. Sadly, most people are blissfully unaware of how their perception of reality is controlled by these means, and this species as a whole falls prey to emotional manipulation as the mechanism that governs their decisions in virtually all matters.

Few people indeed are willing to admit that they are controlled by their emotions, or that their emotions can be manipulated through propaganda and calculated mind-control propaganda techniques, yet this is exactly how humanity has been controlled throughout the ages. From the times of the ancient gods into the present era, creating emotional reactions in the human herds is how humanity has been herded, ruled and manipulated. The person of wisdom sees this manipulation for what it is and rises above it.

When Buddha taught about human suffering he was not referring to the poor, the diseased or the downtrodden. He was referring to the suffering of human consciousness enslaved in the first cognition world of overly-excited, reactive human emotions controlled by the ego virus and its world of illusionary perceptions. It is in this perceptual world of consensus reality, what Buddha referred to as *maya* (illusion), that we find the basis of all human suffering. Those who try to follow the teachings of Buddha to this day have still not realized the true meaning of Nirvana, or the second cognition. Instead his students throughout the ages used first cognition interpretations of the poor and downtrodden as the sufferers and preach doctrines of compassion for these people, and its leaders are just as lost in the first cognition world of illusion as is the Dalai Lama, who by his own admission is a Marxist. They seek and preach a phantasmagorical world of happiness and *bliss* that the true person of wisdom knows does not exist as it is presently understood through bastardized and corrupted first cognition add-ons and misinterpretations of the teachings of Buddha. The only bliss achievable to the individual is the bliss attained through transcending first cognition tyranny and freeing one's mind from the illusion and the control of the false ego virus. When this happens then true silence of the mind occurs and the individual no longer suffers from the poisons of the first cognition world of false perceptions, or *maya*.

The ego virus, what I refer to as the hapiym virus (Hacker Program In Your Mind), is the root cause of all human suffering. This hapiym virus over-amplifies our emotions and makes it easier to control the masses through its infectious qualities.

Because psychology has not fully looked into the reality of this invisible and infectious virus, its effects go unnoticed and the world is blinded by these effects and calls it 'human nature'. Carl Jung tried to classify the effects of the virus as the 'collective unconscious', and I went to great lengths describing this virus and how it operated in my book *The Energetic War Against Humanity: The 6,000 Year War Against Human Cognitive Advancement.* It is easy to deny such things because humanity thrives on denial in the first cognition system of awareness. Denial is the safe-haven of the ego virus and it blinds people from seeing what is right before their eyes, particularly if the information goes against their cultural programming or individual belief system.

Fear is the enforcement mechanism of the virus and it plays human emotions like a violin in order to protect its domain; the human ego. Fear is what makes people deny the truth, for to admit the truth means that their cherished cultural, religious or political beliefs and traditions would have to be tossed out the window in the face of this truth. Fear is what makes every human a cognitive policeman of their fellow beings, striving to keep the consensus reality in place and unchallenged. To move into the second cognition state of higher human awareness one must transcend these fears, and there is nary a person who attained real wisdom who did not teach this same principle that fear must be overcome.

Most fears are based on nothing more than emotional discomfort and the fear of things that 'might' happen. As human beings, our consciousness is shaped by our experiences, which leave emotional imprints that shape our emotional reactions.

Traumatic situations of every degree create an imprint that the hapiym virus calls up as an emotionally-triggered response every time we find ourselves in a similar situation to the original programmed imprint. Through such programming, we are all living our lives in the past, ever reliant on bad experiences from our past to keep those fears in place in our present. To transcend into higher level second cognition awareness and true wisdom, one must break this cycle of repetitive fear programming by facing our fears and defeating them once and for all. When this is accomplished, and it can be, the wise person truly transcends the phantom of programmed fear of this kind. They are no longer controlled by the fear generated by the hapiym virus or its ego programming.

It is this over-emotional reactivity that psychologists call 'human nature', and they are as unaware of the effects of the virus in their own minds as they are within the minds of their clients. Instead, they use the scientific method of observation and measurability to try and reach theoretical conclusions about what they have accepted as human nature. Since everyone on the planet was infected by the hapiym virus without exception, they can only observe the symptomatology of the virus without ever understanding the root cause of this cognitive disease.

Because everyone generally reacts in similar manners to the same stimuli, they have classified this as human nature without moving beyond the symptomatology to see the disease itself. To gain true wisdom and freedom of consciousness one must eradicate the symptoms of the virus to find the real person inside that has been overlaid with this virus mimic of human consciousness. This explains why every genuine teacher of second cognition wisdom has taught that the ego must be transcended to find true cognitive freedom and true wisdom. There is nothing mystical about such an enterprise. It has nothing to do with God or the Divine or some presumed idea of joining with a singular consciousness that rules the universe. It requires gut-wrenching work and fortitude which most people are lacking because of their fears. Anything that tries to pass itself off as wisdom without these principles is simply intellectual philosophizing and nothing more.

3. The Peace of Wisdom

One of the qualities generally attributed to the wise sage is that of being peaceful and not subject to wild emotional swings. The Stoics, who were probably influenced in part by Buddhist thinking migrating to the West, sought this type of emotional equanimity through their own practices of self-discipline which, in this author's view, amounted to nothing more than repressing what they thought were negative emotions. Forced emotional repression through any form of discipline does not qualify as transcending these emotions, but only puts on a false mask of equanimity by studiously burying one's undesired emotions. We see a similar form of emotional manipulation by many new agers who seek to constantly remain in a state of 'love and light' through similar practices of emotional repression, and not too successfully I might add, through my own observations over the years.

Repression of emotions through mental discipline doesn't bring one to a true state of inner peace because one must always use mental discipline to keep those emotions and desires in check. The emotions are not transcended and brought into balance, but take constant attention to keep them repressed, giving only the superficial appearance of stoic balance. With Stoicism, we find the intellectual engagement based on reason and logic, and it became the fascination of the elite classes of philosophers, believing that virtue and ethics were the highest ideals to be attained through intellectual disciplines and emotional repression. This is a first cognition misinterpretation of what Buddha taught as Nirvana, and it is a prime example of how intellectuals throughout the ages have reached erroneous conclusions about overcoming the ego to find second cognition balance.

Regardless of how second cognition perception is explained to a person functioning in first cognition awareness, there is a cognitive disconnect where understanding it is concerned. There is no comparative basis in the first cognition world of over-amplified emotions to understand genuine emotional balance other than achieving a faux balance based on the repression of emotions to create a false state of balance.

The world of the first cognition is over-burdened with rules and regulations, morals and ethics, and other concepts of intellectual superiority governed by the perceptions of the ego, and a humanity controlled by these limited ego perceptions ruled by its emotions. The ego, infected by the hapiym virus, is always over-inflated and self-centered. Every person, controlled by their hapiym-infected ego, is the center of their own universe. This individual perceptual universe is governed by beliefs that the individual embraces and uses to define itself in comparison to other egos with which it is surrounded. Things like moral dictates, concepts of virtue, holiness or intellectual superiority are all tools the hapiym virus uses to bolster every ego in every human being, and every one of these perceptions is governed by external sources that mandate these beliefs. Either some God or holy book mandates these beliefs and governs the individual's behaviors, or they are handed down by authority figures who feel they are qualified to make such mandates on the rest of the human species. It is few humans indeed throughout the ages who have overcome this mass perception to become a truly independent and free individual, setting their own moral or ethical guidelines despite what the mass perception and the consensus reality dictates.

Mass consensus in a belief system of morals and dogmas does not mean that these belief systems are inherently correct. It only means that everyone agrees to abide by rules established by others and ostracize anyone who doesn't agree with the mass consensus perception. This is the herd mentality presented to humanity whose mind has been infected with a pernicious virus that thrives in a hive environment. To the hapiym virus, there is always strength in numbers, never in the individual who stands apart from the herd. Look at any culture on this planet and you will find that this is the rule and not the exception. Compliance and conformity are the rule of the day within any human herd. Granted, there are multitudes of differing herds, but solidarity and conformity to its own rules within each selective herd is the mandate, and the different herds will not draw the line where it comes to eliminating other herds to spread their ideologies and make their own herds larger. Above all, religions have been the worst perpetrators of mandated herd compliance and conformity over the ages of humanity. Political ideologies run a close second place to conformity of thinking produced by force and murder or punishment for non-compliance. The modern Globalist agenda is just the latest example of forced compliance to a planetary herd agenda being foisted on humanity by a cadre of self-proclaimed elite who are the Fabian Society and their multitudes of think tanks, banking allies, the United Nations, and tens of thousands of tax free foundations worldwide.

The compliant herds have separated themselves into varying camps of opposition, playing right into the hands of the global psychological manipulators and laying the foundation for revolutions, the destruction of nations, and the very real possibility of a global war using religion, once again, to fulfill the agenda of divide and conquer. Their motto is *Ordo ab Chao,* or Order out of Chaos. Naturally, they are creating the chaos through controlling the media and spouting propaganda as psychological manipulation over the masses, and an emotionally charged humanity can't see the manipulation taking place through these methods. Their 'order', is a Marxist-based ideology for world government of this design.

Through abusing mass psychology via media manipulation, the hapiym-infected human species continues to have its consciousness molded like clay in the hands of these artful technicians of tyranny. The wise sage sees this manipulation and has risen above the cognitive tyranny to free their own consciousness from such base methods of psychological emotional manipulation. The one with true wisdom can see the chaos for what it is and no longer participates in the first cognition illusion. The person of wisdom has the pragmatism to face this world without fear and without being controlled by overactive emotions. One can live in this world but not be a part of the world that is controlled by these factors. This is true balance and peace, not some ditzy concept of perpetual happiness and bliss. The truly wise individual is highly pragmatic and doesn't fall for escapist mystical fantasies, chasing rainbows of bliss or heavenly greener pastures that only exist in the imagination of first cognition perceptions.

At the time that Buddha lived, he was witness to an expanding, war-driven Hindu religion that eventually dispossessed his family because his father refused to comply with the expanding herd religion's compliance mandates of the era. This is what caused the Indian prince Guatama to go into his own dark abyss period of cognitive dissonance that eventually led him to his own discoveries about the second cognition and ultimately share his teachings with others. Buddha eventually made serious inroads against the Hindu status quo, and Hindu literature still shows the mandate that all Buddhists must be killed as a threat to their religion and their gods. After Buddha's death, the intellectual philosophical classes infiltrated his teachings and poisoned and corrupted them with first cognition perceptions about compassion, perpetual bliss, monasticism, and eventually turned his teachings into just another institutionalized herd religion.

Five hundred years later, the man known to us a Jesus again attempted to teach humanity about second cognition consciousness, and once again, first cognition religious tyrants turned his messages into a murderous religious dependency called Christianity. The heretics to the mainstream, pro-Roman Pauline doctrine were hunted down and killed, or forced to convert under threat of death, and this pernicious first cognition ideology, laden with shame, guilt, ambiguous moral mandates and justifiable murder has wrought more bloodshed over the last 1,700 years than

Christian adherents are willing to admit. Christianity's history is not that of a religion of peace any more than Islam or Hinduism. The claims of any religion about being 'peaceful' religions based on deified justification of mass murder belies each of these religious ideologies as nothing more than cognitive scams used to justify wholesale herd compliance to their own versions of consensus reality and cognitive control.

The Marxist socialism of the Fabian Society is just another form of political religion, as accurately noted by Gustave Le Bon in his book *The Psychology of Socialism*. The advancement of Fabian socialism on a global scale is no different than the spread of any religion, and the tactics of propaganda used to push this elitist agenda are no different than those used to advance religious ideologies throughout the ages. Control human emotions, formulate and push your own alleged moral mandates, sell your product through any means necessary (including violence), until the masses cave in to the consensus tyranny. Eliminate all heretics to the doctrine until the elite controllers have a compliant populace willing to follow the doctrine like drones. This is the living legacy of humanity functioning in the first cognition reality, and a pragmatic historical analysis proves this time and again as the repetitive pattern that human consciousness can't break free from, for the simple reason that it chooses to not do so.

The pragmatic person of wisdom can see this cognitive tyranny and is not afraid to admit it. They are not afraid to call a spade a spade, nor do they cower in fear from the tableau called the 'human condition'. The wise person can have a sense of compassion over the untapped potential of an entire species lost in a cognitive illusion, but feeding that illusion by offering compassion and emotional support to the cognitive tyranny is not part of their second cognition perceptions. The truly wise person realizes that only humanity can change itself, and emotional displays of 'faux compassion', as don Juan called it, are only going to feed those lost in the first cognition illusion. In psychological terminology, this is called enabling.

The so-called human condition is nothing more than a self-imposed tyranny of herd compliance, conformity and comfortability attained through ages of cognitive programming. The truly sad part of all this is that it can be changed for any individual that truly wants to break free of the illusion and transcend all the cultural programming that holds each individual prisoner in their own minds. A lot of people are starting to observe what can be seen from the second cognition about this condition of mental slavery about which I speak, however, they turn their sights to the "ancient" teachings that masquerade as wisdom trying to keep these traditions alive in modern times. What humanity fails to understand is that 'conventional wisdom' doesn't matter if it is 50 years old or 5,000 years old. It has never, and will never, bring humanity at large to a greater level of cognitive awareness. What humanity can become through this cognitive transition is currently unimaginable to human perception operating in the first cognition, for it lacks both what Friedrich Nietzsche called *The Will to Power* and the willingness to imagine anything greater than what it perceives as knowledge and wisdom within this limited perceptual illusion. Humanity demands holding itself prisoner to its own limited form of consciousness, refusing to see anything beyond the desires of the collective herd ego, regardless of which particular herd the individual is a member.

Friedrich Nietzsche is probably one of the most misunderstood philosophers of modern times because, as with his second cognition forerunners, first cognition intellectualism does not reach far enough to comprehend what he tried to relate in *Thus Spoke Zarathustra.* For all intents and purposes, Nietzsche himself was the character of Zarathustra in that work; an individual who perceived the fallacy of the first cognition perceptual world filled with slaves to not only the individual ego, but slaves to the group ego of herd mentality. Nietzsche's Zarathustra saw the herds as brain dead and controlled by fear and traditions, giving up their lives for erroneous beliefs in God and a magical hereafter, thereby relinquishing all responsibility as caretakers of the planet we inhabit. Nietzsche's Zarathustra saw a different and more fulfilling road for humanity to follow. In *Thus Spoke Zarathustra* he wrote:

> *"I teach you the overman. Man is something to be surpassed. What have you done to surpass him?*
>
> *All beings thus far have created something beyond themselves: and you want to be the ebb of this great tide, and even return to the beast rather than surpass man?*
>
> *What is the ape to man? A laughing-stock or a painful embarrassment. And just the same*

shall man be to the overman: a laughing-stock or a painful embarrassment.

You have made your way from worm to man, and much inside you is still worm. Once you were apes, and still man is more of an ape than any of the apes.

Even the wisest among you is only a conflict and mix of plant and ghost. But do I bid you become ghosts or plants?

Behold, I teach you the overman!

The overman is the meaning of the earth. Let your will say: The overman shall be the meaning of the earth!

I appeal to you, my brothers, remain true to the earth, and do not believe those who speak to you of otherworldly hopes! Poisoners are they, whether they know it or not.

Despisers of life are they, decaying and poisoned themselves, of whom the earth is weary: so let them pass away!"

The wisdom in these passages is still not understood in the first cognition world. Hitler took Nietzsche's writings and came up with the first cognition concept of a ruling Aryan race of alleged supermen, yet a full study of Nietzsche reveals that he detested the idea of an Aryan supremacy, noting particularly the translation of the Sanskrit word *arya* to mean 'the owners'. Nietzsche's 'overman' is not this first cognition tyrannical Aryan monstrosity pushed forth by Hitler's socialist ideology, but represents a cognitively advanced human being who can transcend the failings of the ego as well as transcending the herd mentality and brainwashing present in the human species through religions, cultural programming and traditions that have remained unchanged for thousands of years.

Nietzsche further noted that:

> *"Man is a rope stretched between animal and overman - a rope over an abyss.*
>
> *A dangerous crossing, a dangerous on-the-way, a dangerous looking back, a dangerous trembling and stopping.*
>
> *What is great in man is that he is a bridge and not a goal: what can be loved in man is that he is an over-going and a down-going.*
>
> *I love those who know not how to live except as down-goers, for they are the over-goers."*

As one who had experienced second cognition perception, Nietzsche could accurately define humanity functioning in the first cognition world of perception as an unfinished product, lost between being an animal and the second cognition overman. To become a cognitively free individual living with second cognition perception did not require gene-splicing humans with animals, nor seeking to 'improve' humanity through creating cyborg humans in the Fabian Transhumanist mold, but is found in shifting human consciousness into a state of cognitive maturity rather than the cognitive adolescence that the first cognition reality provides. In order to achieve this crossing over this abyss, one must 'go under', meaning that the individual must let go of the beliefs and perceptions mandated by the herds which keeps humanity prisoner within a rigid, and very limited state of perceptual awareness.

To attain the peace of wisdom one must cross the abyss of letting go of what they perceive reality to be, for in doing so, as each belief and erroneous perception is eradicated, the emotions associated with defending these beliefs come into harmony and balance of their own accord. Simply replacing one belief with another may bring a sense of first cognition emotional peace when one settles into a new herd, but the emotions controlled by the ego are still over-active and control the individual. This is not the peace of the sage who truly possesses wisdom.

One cannot step into wisdom without levelling polemic at a system driven and controlled by cognitive tyranny. When people functioning in the first cognition are confronted with truths that their ego and their herd indoctrination disagrees with, silence the messenger is the rule of the day. Within the first cognition reality, defending one's faith, whether that is religious, cultural, racial or political faith, is how this system of tyranny protects itself from change. Living comfortable lies is more important than accepting uncomfortable truths. Cognitive laziness and the demand to have things remain the same has been the bane of humanity throughout the ages. Humanity may have advanced the collection of facts that it calls knowledge, but the system of consciousness to use this information has not changed one whit throughout the ages. Even with the notable repeating patterns of history and the ability to categorize, sort and manipulate information to control consciousness, humanity still operates under the illusion that it has free will in the first cognition quagmire of cognitive deception.

The peace of wisdom comes when the individual can see these things for what they are; when they can see through the lies and deceptions and no longer have their consciousness controlled by such tools of tyranny. When the individual no longer has an emotional investment in religious beliefs, political ideologies or any other kind of herd acceptance, then they attain true cognitive freedom. Humanity has had a choice to mature for, at minimum, 2,600 years with the teachings left behind by those who had attained the maturity of human consciousness, yet the defenders of the 'old ways' stand waiting and ready to destroy anything that disrupts the bleak cognitive sameness of their first cognition world. For this reason, until humanity decides to outgrow this gravely outmoded form of consciousness, it will never know any true peace as a species. Humanity is a species that ever yearns for more but is too lazy to bring about the necessary changes to have the world of peace and prosperity available to them come about. Humanity is too set in its ways to let go, and this unwillingness to change may well spell the destruction of the species as its methods to kill each other outweigh the common-sense consciousness needed to change for the better.

4. Explaining the Ego Problem

"What a strange simplification and falsification people live in! The wonders never cease, for those who devote their eyes to such wondering. How we have made everything around us so bright and easy and free and simple! How we have given our senses a carte blanche for everything superficial, given our thoughts a divine craving for high-spirited leaps and false inferences! – How we have known from the start to hold on to our ignorance in order to enjoy a barely comprehensible freedom, thoughtlessness, recklessness, bravery, and joy in life; to delight in life itself! And, until now, science could arise only on this solidified, granite foundation of ignorance, the will to know rising up on the foundation of a much more powerful will, the will to not know, to uncertainty, to untruth!"

Friedrich Nietzsche – Beyond Good and Evil

What Nietzsche is describing in the foregoing quote is an accurate description of the first cognition perceptual world controlled by the ego. It is a perceptual world whose foundations are based in ignorance, or as Nietzsche noted, "the will to not know, to uncertainty, to untruth." The ego will claim to desire truth, but the only 'truth' it wants to hear is the truth that confirms its own illusions and beliefs about itself and its world. Anything that contradicts these presumed truths adopted by the individual ego will be shouted down and denied because it does not conform to the perceptual world created by the ego illusion.

In our modern technological era, the glitter of scientific gewgaws bedazzles the consciousness of the ego, keeping it pacified with the latest cell phone apps, home entertainment appliances, and carnival lights to dazzle the weak-minded escapist mentality that is the first cognition. For the more serious addicts, those who crave violence, we have Hollywood productions and video games to fulfill the fantasy need for violence without being violent, or technological weapons of war so we can better kill off other members of our species from afar without getting our clothes bloody or suffer physical harm. At the bottom rung of the first cognition herd hierarchy we find the street gang criminal elements who demand the death of another person in order to join the ranks of these ego-driven miscreants. The high end of the herd hierarchy is populated with the true psychopaths like the leaders of the Fabian Society and the lackeys they help put into political offices worldwide. There is no level of human culture anywhere on the planet that is not governed and controlled by people with superficial ego illusions about themselves, from the individual to the culture itself.

Every individual ego is shaped by its cultural environment and it starts when parents subject their children to their own beliefs, seeking to perpetuate the same programming and brainwashing that made them what they are. What we see in the first cognition world under the influence of the hapiym mind virus is a multigenerational infection being passed from one generation to the next throughout human history. Every parent belongs to one mass ego herd or another, and each of them seeks to indoctrinate their children with the same herd rules that they believe themselves. These patterns of infectious indoctrination are passed from generation to generation and the effects of the virus thrive and grow like a cancer on the consciousness of humanity.

Every bit of 'knowledge' that humanity claims to possess is merely a concatenation of presumed facts based on either mystical beliefs or stark materialistic science. There is very little middle ground between these two extremes, and most assuredly no effort being put forth by humanity to transcend these borders of opposing extremity. These are the corral walls that keep all of humanity's consciousness fenced in to a world of limited perceptions which none can see beyond.

Psychologists are presumably our bellwethers for determining herd sanity and compliance. These arrogant academics feel that they are infinitely qualified to monitor and treat the 'human condition' as presumed experts in their fields. Of psychologists, Nietzsche noted in *Beyond Good and Evil*:

*"All psychology so far has been stuck in moral prejudices and fears: it has not ventured into the depths. To grasp psychology as morphology and the **doctrine of the development of the will to power,** which is what I have done – nobody has ever come close to this, not even in thought: this, of course, to the extent that we are permitted to regard what has been written so far as a symptom of what has not been said until now. The power of moral prejudice has deeply affected the most spiritual world, which seems like the coldest world, the one most likely to be devoid of any presuppositions – and the effect has been manifestly harmful, hindering, dazzling, and distorting."*

What Nietzsche is trying to explain to the reader is that psychology exists in a static environment. It makes all its determinations on the assumption that the symptoms of the hapiym virus are in fact human nature, yet the psychologist is as infected by the mind virus as those they diagnose. To move into the second cognition, through what Nietzsche referred to as *the will to power*, one must break free from this static cognitive environment and morph into a new level of human awareness. This is what he means when he says we should see psychology as morphology. His observations about psychology being 'stuck in moral prejudices and fears' is absolutely correct, and this is why psychology as it is currently practiced as a soft-science will never resolve the symptoms of the human condition, but can only perpetuate it. Psychologists and psychiatrists are in the business of helping hapiym infected egos fit back into their specific cultural herds. They are simply egos trying to repair other egos that they consider broken according to their own professional herd's standards of measurement. It is the blind leading the blind, and transcending the ego is not something that a single practitioner of psychology can assist anyone with. These practitioners can no more explain Nietzsche's concept of *the will to power* through cognitive morphology than any philosopher can. They are all stuck in the same cognitive meat grinder as everyone else, but their professional hubris ensures that their own egos will never admit this fact.

When Buddha crossed the transition point in his own cognitive evolution, the word ego did not exist. Buddha referred to what we now know as the ego as the illusionary 'self'. He taught that all human suffering could be transcended, but unless one understands that it is the illusionary and hapiym-infected ego that is the root of all of humanity's cognitive suffering, his words are lost on first cognition followers. Even practicing Buddhists have not escaped the traps of the ego herd mentality, regardless of their facetious claims that they have transcended ego, or they would not have the need to wear saffron robes and dress alike, cluster in monasteries together and peddle their religion just like any other herd religion. They are all living as much a superficial cognitive illusion as those they profess to have compassion for, with their own egos providing a superior attitude over the lost masses of humanity who do not agree with their teachings.

To evolve yourself into the next level of mature human consciousness, the second cognition and Nietzsche's *overman*, one must transcend all herd consolidation to find true and honest cognitive freedom. As long as you are bound by the mandates of culture and tradition, or are pressured to perform according to rules mandated by the masses to control the individual, you are not truly free. Your consciousness and your actions are dictated by the decisions of other. Your likes and dislikes are only allowed within the herd mandates, and if you are discovered operating outside those mandates, the herd will police you into cognitive oblivion while demanding always that you conform, conform, CONFORM!

Nietzsche accurately reported the path required to overcome the ego beast in our minds in *Beyond Good and Evil* when he wrote:

> *"Independence is an issue that concerns very few people: – it is a prerogative of the strong. And even when somebody has every right to be independent, if he attempts such a thing without **having** to do so, he proves that he is probably not only strong, but brave to the point of madness. He enters a labyrinth, he multiplies by a thousand the dangers already inherent in the very act of living, not the least of which is the fact that no one with eyes will see how and where he gets lost and lonely and is torn limb from limb by some cave-Minotaur of conscience. And assuming a man like this is*

destroyed, it is an event so far from human comprehension that people do not feel it or feel for him: – and he cannot go back again! He cannot go back to their pity again!"

This is the price that everyone must pay for cognitive independence. This is the path of choosing *willful evolution*, and it takes a person who is both brave enough and strong enough to go against consensus reality and the status quo of herd indoctrination, to not only embark on such a journey, but to succeed at it by defeating the mental tyrant that is their own ego. As Nietzsche wrote in *Zarathustra*, it is a perilous going over this abyss and everyone must take this journey on their own, for it is one's own internal will to power that will give them the strength to cross over that abyss to reach the second cognition realm of the *overman*.

The perilousness of this journey is found in the ego's need for herd solidarity and external acceptance to feed itself. Once one starts to starve the ego, the remnants and habits of the hapiym virus seem to amplify, creating hindrances at every turn. Few indeed have the stamina or courage to face down this viral beast that poisons the human mind, and the vast majority turn back in fear along the way, for their ego convinces them that they are not suited for the task and they simply give up on themselves. Humanity has been so programmed with the hapiym virus's hive instinct that few are willing to try and overcome this major survival symptom of the infection to truly learn to walk alone from the herd. This transition in some esoteric traditions is called the dark night of the soul, but it is a long journey and many are deceived along the way, thinking they have walked through this abyss when they have only gone part of the journey.

One who has matured through their own process of willful evolution can see the herd dynamic at play in everyone around them. The by-product of the hapiym virus is hive (herd) conformity and compliance. Although Nietzsche was unaware of, or did not make note of the hapiym mind virus, his consciousness had advanced far enough to see the herd failings in humanity. In *Beyond Good and Evil* he explains exactly what I have tried to relate in my own body of work:

> *"For as long as there have been people, there have been herds of people as well (racial groups, communities, tribes, folk, states, churches), and a very large number of people who obey compared to relatively few who command. So, considering the fact that humanity has been the best and most long-standing breeding ground for the cultivation of obedience so far, it is reasonable to suppose that the average person has an innate need to obey as a type of **formal conscience** that commands: "Thou shalt unconditionally do something, unconditionally not do something," in short: "Thou shalt." This need tries to satisfy itself and give its form a content, so, like a crude appetite, it indiscriminately grabs hold and accepts whatever gets screamed into its ear by*

some commander or another – a parent, teacher, the law, class prejudice, public opinion – according to its strength, impatience, and tension. The oddly limited character of human development – its hesitancy and lengthiness, its frequent regressions and reversals – is due to the fact that the herd instinct of obedience is inherited the best and at the cost of the art of commanding. If we imagine this instinct ever advancing to its furthest excesses, in the end there will be nobody with independence or the ability to command; or, such people will suffer inwardly from bad consciences and need to fool themselves into thinking that they too are only obeying before they are able to command."

Contrary to what some of my readers may think, it was not until I had reached my own similar conclusions on these matters that I delved into Nietzsche's work. I am not Nietzsche's parrot, although the vision of the wise overman sees the same faults with an obedient and ego-controlled humanity in all its fatal glory from generation to generation. This is what represents honest truth-telling and understood wisdom more than all the fanciful intellectual notions of first cognition academic and philosophical speculators throughout the ages. One who possesses true wisdom sees the same cognitive illusion enslaving humanity regardless of which generation they were born into. True wisdom paints the same picture throughout the generations and does not falter or vary except through how the wise individual relates these consistent truths. Wisdom that varies through the ages based on speculation, religious mandates, laws, morals or the popular consent of the times is not genuine wisdom, it is merely accepted opinion masquerading as wisdom. Wisdom is not based on democracy, although this is how the first cognition treats it, with fabricated terms like 'conventional wisdom' used to mask mass herd agreement to describe this fallacious pretender to wisdom.

As Nietzsche accurately observes, obedience is what keeps the varied human herds in line. Every herd has its own set of rules, morals and 'Thou Shalts' to keep its members in line, and every herd has its presumed authorities through which the mandates of obedience are handed down, be they priests, politicians, academics or gurus. Obedience is intimately linked to the authority syndrome and neither can survive without the other. It is only true wisdom that leads people to understand that they are ultimately responsible for themselves and what they do without rules handed down by presumed authorities or reinforced through the obedient herd ego compliance.

Obedience is the easy road, for it takes nothing to obey and walk in lockstep to the orders of authorities, who appear and disappear throughout time leaving the human herds following their mandates long after they are dead. This is particularly true with so-called religious authorities whose presumed mandates by their gods keep human consciousness poisoned and obedient even into this technological age. Religious pretenders to authority are the most dangerous because they hide behind the mask of their imaginary gods, whereas intellectual academic authorities run a close second place hiding behind the mask of their laurels and degrees to give them the presumption of authority. Politicians run a third place to these other two because they play on the public perception using both an intellectual claim to guide their nations and never hesitate to get behind the national religion to align themselves with both sides. Priests, gurus, imams and intellectualists are the seducers of the masses, politicians are the whores whose highest credential is that of the pathological liar.

The evilest perpetrators of the authority syndrome are the psychopathic demagogues, those who can both seduce others and control the whores in politics to do their bidding. If we look at the political spectrum around the world, we find politics driven by demagoguery in every nation, with populists stirring up the masses while the silent manipulators of the Fabian Society play all sides against one another, ultimately seeking total global hegemony with their Marxist socialist ideology. While these Fabian psychopaths disparage Capitalism, and push their Marxist agenda, they are in bed with, and have been for well over a century, the Eastern Establishment bankers who underwrite their socialist agenda. This is what is known as Liberal Capitalism, where there is a perceptual illusion of opposition, but where all sides are controlled by the same psychopathic families, selectively breeding with one another generation after generation through their own ideology of eugenics. Today, there is no difference between Capitalism, as it is practiced, and Communism, except the perception of there being a difference. It is all controlled by the same people and only the perceptual illusion of propaganda presents the facsimile of any real difference.

Humanity, operating under control of the ego mind virus, covers the spectrum of both the authorities and the obedient. It is a self-perpetuating tyranny unimaginable to all except the person who possesses the true wisdom to see the horrible tapestry of the 'human condition' and realize the useless tragedy of it all. Only the person of wisdom has the strength to see these truths and survive in such a carnival of cognitive self-destruction and repeating errors. Viewing these facts, and they are facts, do you still believe that there is safety in numbers beyond one mind-infected herd protecting itself against another, always demanding the status quo based on dried up and meaningless ancient traditions? This is not cognitive evolutionary progress, it is cognitive stagnancy which has turned human consciousness into a toxic cesspool.

Nietzsche was excoriated and vilified for making the statement that "God is dead". The fact is that God, regardless of his name, as envisioned by first cognition perception, never existed as anything beyond an idea for tyranny and authoritarian control, no matter which robes this God chooses to wear. God is not dead, the invisible God who presumptively created everything in existence never existed. God is the greatest authority figure imaginable to a species who demands to be obedient to some authority. Humanity begs to be ruled and subjugated for the simple reason that it refuses to take responsibility for itself. There is no wisdom in this equation, only servitude, and this is what the hapiym virus has given humanity as its gift to the ego; obedience, subservience, and continual destruction throughout the ages. *This* is the real human condition!

5. Confirmation Bias is Willful Ignorance

Confirmation bias, or confirmatory bias, is defined as:

"the tendency to interpret new evidence as confirmation of one's existing beliefs or theories."

In more simplified terms, confirmation bias means that one seeks out, interprets or bends information to fit into a mental box of an individual's personal biases and beliefs. The majority of humanity on this planet lives in a perceptual illusion based on the individual's conditioned cognitive programming, which is a product of cultural programming at all levels of the individual's cognitive ego development. The individual ego gravitates to varying beliefs within these cultural herds and establishes their individual perceptual reality based on these beliefs and embraced ideologies.

The foremost names in the earliest days of the development of the field of Psychology can be found in association with the Society of Psychical Research (SPR), which was intimately co-joined with Madame Helena Blavatsky's Theosophical Society, and out of whose association arose the Fabian Society. Amongst their foremost educational facilities, we find many of these founders of Psychology intimately associated with the London Tavistock Institute of Human Relations, which is reputed to be the foremost training ground for the studies in controlling the human masses through psychological mind control techniques. Sigmund Freud was a member of Tavistock Institute and it is his techniques that became the model for shaping psychological studies through Tavistock Institute.

Through the Fabian Society, the Theosophical Society and Tavistock Institute, we find tens of thousands of tax free organizations funded by the Rockefeller and Ford Foundations, and probably one of the largest trust organizations on the planet, the Lucis Trust, created by Alice and Foster Bailey. Alice Bailey was a member of the Fabian Society who eventually became president of the American branch of the Theosophical Society, and the Lucis Trust organization was originally claimed to have been created to publish Bailey's Theosophical books.

The Theosophical Society, colluding with their Fabian Society counterparts, were responsible for pushing the League of Nations and eventually succeeded in this endeavor with the creation of the United Nations, a charitable trust safely nestled under the Lucis Trust umbrella of organizations that span the globe. The land on which the United Nations is built was provided by the Rockefeller Foundation, and until recently, the Lucis Trust Organization was housed at 666 United Nations Plaza.

All the aforementioned organizations interlink in an incestuous relationship that have secretly colluded together for over a century, working to consolidate all the religio-spiritual traditions, as well as all political traditions, under one tyrannical globalist agenda. Professing Marxist ideologies and hidden goddess worship traditions just now publicly coming to light through the Freemasons, as I reported in my book *We Are Not Alone – Part 3: The Luciferian Agenda of the Mother Goddess*, these organizations are the enigmatic 'deep state' being alluded to in the press, but which the Fabian-Zionist owned media refuses to report truthfully.

Each of these organizations has a heavy investment in using Psychology as a weapon against the rest of humanity through propaganda. The modern New Age Movement is controlled through the organizations created by Lucis Trust and the Theosophical Society, and the Theosophical Society has been working since the late 19th century to homogenize all religious and spiritual traditions into a unified global religion. With Pope Francis being the first Jesuit priest serving as Pope, who also is a proponent of Marxist Liberation Theology, the stage is set for the consolidation for virtually all the world's religions to be folded under one Fabian Marxist banner.

Under close examination, the pacifist doctrines and Marxist revolutionary tactics of the liberal left observed since the 2016 U.S. election debacle, we can see a merging of doctrinal tactics between the Theosophical Society and Fabian Marxist ideologies, funded by George Soros and pushed through the Eastern Establishment university systems which were hijacked by the Fabians early on. Through the takeover of Eastern universities in the USA in the 19th and 20th century, the educational system has become the strongest tool for brainwashing and indoctrinating American youth since the Fabian John Dewey placed his fingerprints on the public-school system. Aside from the largest banks in the U.S., the universities in the American northeast are just another extension of the Fabian Society's Anglo-Eastern Liberal Capitalist Establishment.

These are the ugly truths that the general populace refuses to believe, remaining content to live in their much safer perceptual world of cognitive denial and herd confirmation bias. One of the forerunners in Social Psychology, Wilfred Trotter, observed in his 1916 book, *Instincts of the Herd in Peace and War:*

> *"Each of us has the strongest conviction that his conduct and beliefs are fundamentally individual and reasonable and in essence, independent of external causation, and each is ready, to furnish a series of explanations of his conduct consistent with these principles. These explanations, moreover, are the ones which will occur spontaneously, to the observer watching the conduct of his fellows."*

We find that Trotter's observation is a general truism where the individual is concerned. Each individual believes that they have free will and that the choices they make in life are their own, based on their own individual decisions. The overlooked aspect of this particular belief system is that if all the 'choices' you are given to choose from are dictated by others, what Trotter refers to as 'external causation', how much free will do you really have? Everyone's presumed choices are dictated either by cultural mandates, traditions, religious or political mandate, or smaller peer herd pressures. Whichever herds one belongs to, and a person can be part of a number of different herds within an overarching cultural herd, each herd has its own mandates of conformity, and each herd survives through a form of group confirmation bias. Confirmation bias is acutely driven by emotions and the conviction that one is inherently correct in whatever beliefs they embrace, despite the fact that there may be overwhelming evidence to the contrary. This emotional attachment was noted by Trotter when he wrote in the aforementioned book:

> *"A very little consideration of the problem of conduct makes it plain that it is in the region of feeling, using the term in its broadest sense, that the key is to be sought. Feeling has relations to instinct as obvious and fundamental as are the analogies between intellectual processes and reflex action. . ."*

Trotter realized early on that it is emotions (feeling) that govern the herd mentality where the beliefs of the herd are concerned. To control the herd, one only needs to manipulate people's emotions. What Trotter and others of his ilk failed to realize is that the emotions currently exhibited by humans operating in the first cognition are not instinctual, but are the symptoms of the hapiym virus and its effects on the human mind and emotional physiology. The emotions exhibited by humanity are not genetic, nor are they instinct. They are the *symptoms* of a mimic mind virus that creates over-amplified emotional outbursts and reactions to external stimuli at the drop of a hat.

The Aryan invaders who I exposed in my *We Are Not Alone* three-part additions to *The Evolution of Consciousness* series of books, have been privy to information intentionally kept from the rest of humanity for the last 6,000 years. Trotter reveals a key part of this information when he wrote:

> *"One of the most familiar attitudes was that which regarded the social instinct as a late development. The family was looked upon as the primitive unit; from it developed the tribe, and by the spread of family feeling to the tribe the social instinct arose. It is interesting that the psychological attack upon this position has been anticipated by sociologists and anthropologists, and that it is already being recognized that an undifferentiated horde rather than the family must be regarded as the primitive basis of human society."*

Wilfred Trotter – *Instincts of the Herd in Peace and War* (Public Domain - 1916)

When one can accept the truth that the human race on this planet was created as a slave race to more technologically advanced races of beings from the stars, then Trotter's assertion falls perfectly in line with what I presented in the *We Are Not*

Alone books. Earth humans, at their lab-created inception, were a mass of undifferentiated beasts of burden and a literal food supply to other races of beings who viewed our race as nothing more than bipedal cattle – *man-kine*. Our oldest ancestors come from such ignominious circumstances that the mind rebels to reject this horrible truth. Such an idea shocks our very conscious so much that we, as a species, will believe anything else to avoid facing this horrible truth. The Aryan occupiers of this planet are fully aware of the 'human condition' in this regard and it is one of the most well-kept secrets on the planet. This is why they so cavalierly refer to humanity as 'the herd', and even the Jewish word *goy* translates to mean 'cattle'.

These are the ugly truths that the person of wisdom can see and come to terms with as truth, whereas those lost in the perceptual illusion of first cognition will live with beliefs fabricated by their authoritarian controllers throughout the ages, who established every cultural tradition around the planet. Confirmation bias is the reinforcement mechanism that keeps this perceptual illusion in place, and it is the worst form of willful ignorance and denial that allows these Aryan occupiers, who control humanity to this day, to have the free reign to hold 99% of humanity prisoners through psychological and emotional manipulation and mental subjugation. Wisdom comes when the individual can see these truths and unshackle the chains of cognitive subjugation from their psyche.

When we factor in the effects of the hapiym mind virus that infects every human on this planet, including the Aryan controllers, then Trotter's claims about the undifferentiated herd take on an even more profound meaning. Humanity in and of itself is probably not so mandatorily social as the early psychologists perceived, but humanity has been subconsciously 'socialized' into a collective herd mentality as a direct result of the hapiym hive mind virus that infects our entire species. All of the conjecture about human nature has been put forth by simply observing the effects of the hapiym infection, and the observers themselves are just as infected with this virus as all of humanity. They have sought answers to the 'human condition' by delving into the subconscious mind by using techniques of hypnotism, developed by Franz Mesmer (mesmerism), to tap into what the psychologist Carl Jung referred to as the 'collective unconscious'.

The collective unconscious that Jung sought to understand is the hapiym hive virus, and I explained this in full in my book *The Energetic War Against Humanity: The 6,000 Year War Against Human Cognitive Advancement.* Psychological researchers over the last 100 years have sought to understand the subconscious mind, reaching the erroneous conclusion that the collective unconscious, or subwaking state as the psychologist Boris Sidis called it, is a natural part of the human psyche. Since every human being was infected with this virus, and the fact that the hapiym virus itself masked itself behind the inflated ego, discovering the virus itself as the cause of the human social herding instinct remained undetected by these experts in Psychology. They could observe the socializing and herding habits of the virus, but they could not make the determination that these observed behaviors were not in fact part of human nature, but were the effects of an energetic mental virus that created these behaviors as a symptom of the infection itself. The viral instinct to cluster in hives or herds is the nature of the hapiym infection, and human behavior is dictated by the hive effect in its need to cluster in social herds. This is how the hapiym infection manipulates the consciousness of every infected individual and it keeps its energetic food supply abundant in a herd environment. The food supply of the virus is the energy generated from over-amplified human emotions.

In 1919, the psychologist Boris Sidis released his book *The Psychology of Suggestion,* in which he wrote:

"Suggestibility is the cement of the herd, the very soul of the primitive social group. A herd of sheep stands packed close together, looking abstractedly, stupidly, into vacant space. Frighten one of them; if the animal begins to run, frantic with terror, a stampede ensues. Each sheep passes through the movements of its neighbour. The herd acts like one body animated by one soul. Social life presupposes suggestion. No society without suggestibility. Man is a social animal, no doubt; but **he is social because he is suggestible***. Suggestibility, however, requires disaggregation of consciousness; hence, society presupposes a cleavage of the mind, it presupposes a plane of cleavage between the differentiated individuality and the undifferentiated reflex consciousness, the indifferent subwaking self.* **Society and mental**

epidemics are intimately related / for the social gregarious self is the suggestible subconscious self.

The very organization of society keeps up the disaggregation of consciousness. The rules, the customs, the laws of society are categorical, imperative, absolute. One must obey them on pain of death. Blind obedience is a social virtue. But blind obedience is the very essence of suggestibility, the constitution of the disaggregated subwaking self. Society by its nature, by its organization, tends to run riot in mobs, manias, crazes, and all kinds of mental epidemics.

With the development of society, the economical, political, and religious institutions become more and more differentiated; their rules, laws, by-laws, and regulations become more and more detailed, and tend to cramp the individual, to limit, to constrain his voluntary movements, to contract his field of consciousness, to inhibit all extraneous ideas in short, to create conditions requisite for a disaggregation of consciousness. If, now, something striking fixes the attention of the public a brilliant campaign, a glittering holy image, or a bright "silver dollar" the subwaking social self, the demon of the demos, emerges, and society is agitated with crazes, manias, panics, and mental plagues of all sorts.

With the growth and civilization of society, institutions become more stable, laws more rigid, individuality is more and more crushed out, and the poor, barren subwaking self is exposed in all its nakedness to the vicissitudes of the external world. In civilized society laws and regulations press on the individual from all sides. Whenever one attempts to rise above the dead level of commonplace life, instantly the social screw begins to work, and down is brought upon him the tremendous weight of the socio-static press, and it squeezes him back into the mire of mediocrity, frequently crushing him to death for his bold attempt.

Man's relations in life are determined and fixed for him; he is told how he must put on his tie, and the way he must wear his coat; such should be the fashion of his dress on this particular occasion, and such should be the form of his hat; here must he nod his head, put on a solemn air; and there take off his hat, make a profound bow, and display a smile full of delight. Personality is suppressed by the rigidity of social organization; the cultivated, civilized individual is an automaton, a mere puppet.

Under the enormous weight of the socio-static press, under the crushing pressure of economical, political, and religious regulations there is no possibility for the individual to determine his own relations in life; there is no possibility for him to move, live, and think freely; the personal self sinks, the suggestible, subconscious, social, impersonal self rises to the surface, gets trained and cultivated, and becomes the hysterical actor in all the tragedies of historical life."

(Source - Public Domain - 1919)

Sidis' remarks are startlingly accurate when it comes to describing the human socializing mandates of the hapiym virus infection. His study failed to reach the ultimate cause of his observations in human societies. The reader would be well advised to take note of these observations and gain wisdom from them, for they accurately describe how human cultures and sub-cultures work worldwide without exception. Although he referred to 'mental epidemics' he failed to see the global epidemic created by the hapiym virus itself as the root cause of all his observations. Like every psychologist before or since Sidis shared these observations, they are merely witnessing the symptomatology of the virus without discovering the root cause of humanity's subconscious disease, the hapiym hive virus.

Research by Sidis, Trotter and others over the last century or more have laid out how easy it is to control herd psychology through emotional manipulation. They understand the full nature of confirmation bias and how to keep herd beliefs in place to sow dissent in the varied human cultural and sub-cultural herds in order to keep humanity divided against itself so the Aryan controllers can maintain their positions of authority and power. The human psyche is putty in their hands, and any illusions you may have about possessing any kind of true free will must be tossed out the window when every choice you feel you have, other than perhaps choosing a mate, is controlled and manipulated by others. When all your choices are dictated by others, your own free will choices are limited by your options about what to choose from.

When we gravitate to any collective belief system we become part of that particular herd's group consciousness. We accept their rituals, their habits, their subjugation to their own authority, whether that be an individual or some alleged holy book or constitution, and once one believes these things, people generally try to make everything they look at and perceive fit into the cognitive herd box of 'accepted truths'. By refusing to look beyond their chosen or indoctrinated belief systems, and only seeking to reinforce their own her beliefs through confirmation bias, humanity as a whole remains uninformed of the truth and only builds thicker, more impenetrable mental walls to reinforce their own herd beliefs. This is the nature of the virus infection and it has been the source of warfare throughout recorded history, with one herd always seeking dominance and compliance over those that disagree with its own outlook.

The Yaqui sorcerer Don Juan Matús instructed Carlos Castenada that it takes nothing to read about things with which you agree, but to become a man of knowledge, one must read and research what they don't believe or disagree with to gain wisdom and knowledge. Reinforcing one's individual belief system only leaves one a prisoner to that paradigm, insuring that their consciousness stays under the control of the authority paradigm of the accepted belief. This is what confirmation bias leads to, rigid and unbending thinking and faith in belief systems that are not necessarily the true picture of things the way they are.

Conformation bias is choosing to wear rose-colored glasses to paint one's perceptual world. Nothing exists outside this world of self-reinforced illusion that is not viewed as a threat to this perceived reality, whether this bias is predicated on racial divisions, religious, political, national or cultural lines. Each herd of group consciousness is reinforced by the belief that its views are exclusively correct and that opposing perspectives are only a threat to that group's status quo. All the skilled psychological manipulator needs to do to direct these herds is to fill their heads with propaganda and make them feel targeted, and make them emotionally uncomfortable to create mobs, riots, panics and wars. This is the basis of Sidis' observations, as well as Gustave Le Bon's when he first posited the theory of Crowd Psychology. This not only illustrates how easy it is to manipulate all of humanity, but also how it is being done day in and day out everywhere in the world.

Confirmation bias creates both individual and herd solidarity which is each herd's social environment. This is the true meaning of Fabian Marxist Socialism, manipulating all of humanity through creating opposition to every herd on all sides so all of humanity feels threated by the notorious 'others' who don't believe as they do. Through such manipulation by control of the media, the political, educational, religious and cultural brainwashing of the herds, the Fabian controllers play human consciousness like a discordant symphony, and the average person has no idea that they are being manipulated by having their emotions influenced in this manner.

Every herd functions by the external validation of the other herd members, reinforcing confirmation bias that their cause is ultimately the right one, and many are willing to die for these beliefs rather than question whether they are correct or not. Defending the belief through confirmation bias only more deeply embeds the psychological programming of the group consciousness. This is what makes human behavior under the effects of the hapiym virus so sickeningly predictable and easy to manipulate. The person who can see this manipulation and transcend it is the only one who is truly free and can evolve their consciousness beyond these manageable psychological constraints. These are the people who possess true wisdom and who are no longer ruled by confirmation bias and the conventional wisdom that supports the fallacies of selective beliefs of the varied herds.

To move into the second cognition, one must transcend all of their own programming and see the world for what it is and how humanity is being manipulated. The only way out of the first cognition mental prison, controlled by the symptoms of the hapiym virus and its unruly manipulation of human emotions, is to decide to willfully evolve your own consciousness. There is no free golden ticket that is going to give this cognitive freedom to you, you have to claim it for yourself. You can't gain this freedom so long as you are a slave to the ideologies of others and ages old, worn out traditions of herd sameness. If you want security in a social setting, then staying a member of your selected herds is the way to maintain your cognitive status quo, and you will never be a free individual so long as you bend your knees at altars erected by others. Buddha, Jesus, Nietzsche and don Juan all taught these same principles in their own manner, and after 2,500 years, humanity still refuses to listen and grow beyond their cognitive comfort zones of exclusive correctness in their beliefs and their herd environments. Cognitively speaking, humanity is still cattle to the manipulators of this planet, nothing but herds to be managed and manipulated, and it will remain this way so long as people refuse to change themselves for the better. This is true wisdom and humanity exhibits very little of it, which is why it stays on a course of species self-destruction if it doesn't change direction in the very near future.

6. Becoming a Free Individual

The aim of your process for growing into a person of wisdom is to become a free individual, an individual whose consciousness is not controlled by the mandates of others based on collective herd compliance built on faulty perceptions and limited beliefs. In order to accomplish this the individual is going to have to challenge everything they believe and weigh it against larger truths that will often contradict what a person thinks they know. In challenging these belief systems, the individual is equally challenging themselves, as the beliefs become part of what shaped the perceptual reality of the individual personality. This personality is the faux ego of the hapiym virus overlaid onto human consciousness and it keeps everyone aligned with their particular herds out of fear. This is why every teacher of genuine wisdom taught that the false self, or ego, must be challenged and transcended to find true cognitive freedom. I covered this process extensively in *Demystifying the Mystical.*

Friedrich Nietzsche was not the least bit arrogant when he wrote in *Ecce Homo:*

> *"Among my writings my Zarathustra stands by itself. With this book I have given*

mankind the greatest gift it has ever been given. This book, with a voice that carries over millennia, is not only the highest book that there is, the true mountain-air book — the whole fact of man lies at a tremendous distance beneath it — it is also the deepest book, born out of the innermost abundance of truth, an inexhaustible well into which no bucket descends without coming up filled with gold and goodness. Here it is not a "prophet" who speaks, not one of those horrible hybrids of sickness and will to power people call founders of religions. Above all, one must correctly hear the tone that issues from this mouth, this halcyon tone, so as not to do pitiful injustice to the sense of its wisdom."

Naturally, the arrogant ego of the intellectual will project its own shortcomings onto a man of wisdom who is merely making a truthful statement about his work. Neither Buddha, Jesus or don Juan apologized for what they taught from their positions as men of wisdom who had transcended the petty intellectualized ego consciousness of the hapiym virus. Only an ego can fail to understand a statement of truth for what it is and cast aspersions for such plain truthful language, calling it arrogance because the ego lacks the capacity to understand the words or the meaning of such a statement. Only the arrogance of an ego can reach such an erroneous conclusion and hold itself somehow superior to concepts it can't understand. The hapiym infected ego is always right when it comes to protecting its own turf, and this especially applies when it encounters truth that contradicts its own perceptual reality.

The hapiym virus, and you the reader, are a collection of labels and definitions. Your false ego identity is little more than a walking set of descriptions that identify who you are by what you believe. I am a Christian or a Muslim. I am a Republican, a Liberal, a Social Democrat, a Left-Centrist, a Hindu, a Catholic, a Protestant, an Accountant, a Scientist, an Educator, a Male, Female, Chinese, American, Philippino, Australian, a Shaman, a Guru, a Protestant, a Mormon, a member of a Union, and the list of descriptions used to label yourself goes on and on. This is what don Juan meant when he taught that we live in a world of description.

People identify themselves according to their trades, vocations, accomplishments (such as college degrees of presumed mastery, or public awards and trophies), titles of rank, and feats of physical prowess as in the fields of sports. Every one of these aspects of who you think you are is simply a label that the hapiym ego virus folds into the faux identity that makes you believe it is you. Each human being is nothing more than a superficial collection of labels that it uses to identify itself to others. Under the authority syndrome, the higher the presumed rank of the label, the more perceived respect one gets from those who cannot make equal claims to such labeling and personal descriptions.

Due to the infection of the hapiym hive virus, one must always seek approval in the eyes of others for their superficial personality of labels and self-description to be validated by other herd/hive members. The measure of one's worth is always gauged by the response of the external world and what people think of you. This is not just a Western cultural failing, it is global in scope and is found in every culture on this planet. Social (herd) compliance is the norm in every culture, regardless of which rules each herd uses to control its individual members. Group compliance is always the mandate, and not only the authority figures of each individual herd enforce tribal customs and taboos, for every herd member is expected to comply with outcasting or punishing the violators of these laws, rules and customs. There is absolutely no room for a genuinely free thinking, autonomous individual within these ranks, and therefore no genuine cognitive freedom in any kind of herd setting. All one finds is a faux sense of freedom within the cognitive corrals of the specific herd mandates, i.e. you have freedom so long as you do as the herd says.

The problem with humanity becomes evident when we grow the wisdom to finally recognize that all we have is competing herds clustered together mandating their own individual herd rules, and perpetually in competition with, and in opposition to, any other herd that doesn't agree with their own specific mandates. This is the basis of every war throughout recorded human history, and the over-amplified emotions of the masses, induced by the hapiym viral infection, ensures that humanity stays malleable and manipulable through playing on any given herd's paranoia or sense of righteous indignation. Humanity leads with its emotions, not any sense of wisdom. Genuine wisdom must acknowledge the truth of these observations and transcend these cognitive barriers, whereas conventional wisdom only enforces the beliefs to the contrary, calling it 'human nature'.

The true wise man can see through all these descriptions and labels and see the utter cognitive folly under which humanity is governed and controlled. The truly wise individual can see through the masquerade of the ego and defeat all the habits instilled by the hapiym virus and set their consciousness free from this cognitive tyranny. To do less only leaves one a prisoner to the effects of the virus itself.

Wisdom does not reside in reciting platitudes of presumed wisdom, nor is it found in seeking to solve imponderable mystical riddles that have no coherent answers. These things are only a semblance of false wisdom to engage the curiosity of the thinking ego intellect and nothing more. True wisdom is pragmatic and doesn't rely on fanciful notions about prophecies or any form of divine collaboration with long dead mystical masters or mystical concepts of god. Such ideas lie in the realm of the ego's dependency on some higher authority to which it can pass on responsibility for its own actions, and blame as the reason for the individual's personal shortcomings. If you don't get what you want out of life, one can always shirk personal responsibility and say, "It is God's will." This is pure escapist thinking and the responsibility of the individual disappears in the face of such faulty beliefs and blame-laying.

The sad testimony of first cognition human consciousness is that is falls prey to a preference for magical beliefs more than pragmatism, and even the realm of modern science is reliant on the 'magic' of first cognition observation and translating of presumed facts from a materialistic point of view. Science is based purely on a five-sense level of perception and will admit nothing that exists beyond this rigid, yet very limited, form of perception. Within the realm of science, those who profess superiority of their trade are still slaves to a cognitive system of limited perception that refuses to see beyond its own tunnel-vision view of reality. Although science claims to be more pragmatic than religions and mysticism, its system of measurement is firmly rooted in a very limited perspective of nothing existing that can't be measured and quantified through physical means. Unfortunately, consciousness is one thing that the pillars of science have yet to find the origin of. By their system of measurement, consciousness should not exist because it can't be registered on some meter or viewed under a microscope. Within this realm of immeasurable, non-material things, we also find human emotions, the effects of which can be observed, but which can't be defined or measured through materialist scientific instruments.

From one end of this spectrum to the other, first cognition awareness only offers limited perception, and neither the extremes of these poles, nor any point in between, offers humanity any direction to evolve into the next level of its cognitive evolution. Everything remains static where human consciousness is concerned in the first cognition, and only intellect and invention provides the semblance of any kind of perceived advancement. Regardless of our inventiveness in creating new technological toys to distract our egos, or the production of better weapons with which we can kill more people in a sterilized remote fashion, human consciousness has not progressed in over 6,000 years.

Human consciousness is still as barbaric as that of our ancestors, and not a single advancement has occurred to move that state of consciousness forward in all those millennia.

The symptoms of the hapiym virus demand conformity, herd solidarity, obedience to authority, adherence to rules, traditions and ongoing cultural mandates to provide a semblance of comfort to the dependent ego. Humans are taught to fit in, not challenge city hall; to stick with tradition because it has always been that way. Don't break the rules and never make a spectacle of yourself by going against the herd norms. At the base of all these cultural mandates you find fear as the catalyst to keep the rogue free thinker in check. The individual is always secondary to the herd, and this is exactly how the hapiym virus was designed as the infectious agent that it was. The individual can believe anything they want, so long as it complies with some herd mandate somewhere within its identity criteria. The individual doesn't know who they are unless there is a label for the ego to identify itself to others as its mark of personal distinction within any given herd.

The hapiym virus hive instinct can't mind its own business, for the acts of the individual are a merely reflection of the herd itself. In this regard, no virus-infected herd is content to manage their own affairs and not work to dictate their beliefs on others. Through the political processes the different herds elect who they believe will give them what they want in opposition to what a different herd wants. Whenever any particular herd comes to power under the influence of the public opinion of the 'majority', that herd gets to make the rules and laws and impose them on all those who oppose their particular ideology. This is nothing but sanctified mob rule, and when you throw the element of religious ideologies into the political mix, the individual is always threatened.

Using the belief in the legitimacy of alleged 'holy books', every vice one can imagine gets turned into a criminal offense to the believers of the specific religion of the majority. The following excerpt comes from an essay by a little known 19th century American philosopher named Lysander Spooner in his essay *Vices Are Not Crimes,* written in 1875:

"It is a maxim of the law that there can be no crime without a criminal intent; that is, without the intent to invade the person or property of another. But no one ever practices a vice with any such criminal intent. He practices his own vice for his own happiness solely, and not for any malice towards others.

Unless this clear distinction between vices and crimes be made and recognized by the last, there can be on earth no such thing as individual right, liberty, or property; no such things as the right of one man to the control of his own person or property, and the corresponding co-equal rights of another man to the control of his own person or property.

For a government to declare a vice a crime, and punish it as such, is an attempt to falsify the very nature of things. It is as absurd as it would be to declare truth to be falsehood, or falsehood truth."

These are very wise words that the herds of humanity have still not embraced. The nature of the hapiym infection keeps everyone from minding their own business and making everyone's business their own. This is particularly true when it comes to the area of sex and sexual orientation, where one's personal behavior has been governed by outlawing a personal sexual preference because some religious segment of the population finds offense with what it disagrees with as 'normal' sexual activity.

What people do together in their own homes is no one else's concern, regardless of what some religious book mandates or what 'herd norms' dictate for conformist compliance. I use sex and sexual orientation as an example strictly to poke the reader's sensitivities. If you are offended by someone else's adult sexual preferences, and that person is not intruding into your life to make you do what they choose to do, their personal choices are not your concern, nor that of a government or a religious body of arbitrary morals and rules. Their personal choices are not criminal just because you are part of a herd that feels offended because they do not conform to your particular herd's mandates of 'acceptable' behavior. You may be offended by it, but if someone is not trespassing on your person or your property, it's none of your goddamn business what they do. This is wisdom and common sense. The world would be a much better place without meddling 'do-gooders' of every variety, each with a specific banner to wave, to get their own herd's desires shoved down everyone else's throats.

Common sense must also weigh in on this subject where children are concerned, for they do not have the maturity to make rational decisions in any respect. The problem with most religionists is that if one defends the rights of consenting adults to do what they want in the privacy of their own home, the next phantasmagorical leap in illogic is that you sanction pedophilia and child abuse. This is the nature of the offended party in virtually every case. Logic and reason are suspended in the face of the fear called 'what if'. Fear is always the governor that controls the herd and mandates compliance with herd dictates, no matter the issue at hand that promotes this fear. Every gay or lesbian individual is not inherently a pedophile, and the leap of illogic to reach such a conclusion defies reason, but it does generate an irrational fear that creates more herd solidarity within the minds of those who believe such nonsense.

This is why every wise person observed that fear must be overcome in order for one to find wisdom. The fear of change or the fear of the unknown is what drives every herd. This fear of things that 'might be' is enough to control humanity and it is this type of 'what if' fear that keeps humanity as cognitive slaves to this day. Every rigid rule you can imagine is one predicated on fear, whose cousin is doubt. Fear and doubt rule human consciousness, and it is these two elements that keep humanity's consciousness paralyzed like a deer caught in a car's headlights on a road at night.

Fear controls humanity, and fear is the driver behind every individual's sense of self-righteousness in the face of those with opposing ideologies. Fear of 'the other' makes the hapiym-infected ego puff up and bluster about its own superiority over those who threaten it and its herd. The wise individual sees all this fallacious ego posturing by a humanity that demands to stay the same, locked in traditions not of their making, following rules, laws and moral dictates not of their making, and beating their breast and bleating how free they are when they have never had a real moment of cognitive freedom their entire lives. "Don't confuse me with the facts, I know what I believe!" Beliefs can melt away quicker than butter on a hot summer day if you have the courage to face the fallacy of them, which very few people have the courage or desire to do. Humanity lives in a Chicken Little world where the sky is ever falling on one issue or another. It truly is a tragic way to live, and even harder for the person of wisdom to observe when they know there is a saner way to live without fear and all this conflict.

Lysander Spooner has been classified an anarchist. Anarchy is always the label used against an individual who does not flow with the herd, an individual who often exhibits the responsibility to govern his or her own behaviors without having those behaviors dictated by external sources to coerce one into herd compliance. I am not talking about the Marxist version of anarchist as revolutionary, for there is no conscience or responsibility found in anyone who would trespass on another person or their property to push forward a political cause. Admittedly, Spooner was a radical anarchist when it came to the subject of abolition leading up to the American Civil War, but he wrote against slavery rather than starting a revolution.

Spooner wrote against the power of the fictional entity called the State, and how the State is always the offended party whenever crimes are determined. In the present governments of the invisible and non-existent States worldwide, the laws are designed as preventative measures, based on the circumstance that if you do such and such a thing, you 'might' possibly, maybe, umm, under the right conditions, cause harm to another. There is never an injured party in laws of prevention based on potential 'might be's'. Only the invisible State can be an offended party where no offense yet exists. Under Common Law, there must always be an injured party or else there is no crime. Since the State does not exist as anything more than a herd-accepted invisible concept of authority, it can never be victimized or harmed, but the State, in itself, through those who represent the authority of the State, can cause incalculable harm to its populace, and it always does so through legislative mandates and policing actions to enforce its will. Spooner did numerous essays on the State and the court systems that deserve a critical examination by those who can move beyond their indoctrinated herd mandates and see the failure present in human consciousness operating in the first cognition realm of authoritarian dependency.

Later in his essay, Spooner makes this cogent observation which I feel needs to be shared here:

> *"Vices are usually pleasurable, at least for*
> *the time being, and often do not disclose*

themselves as vices by their effects until after they have been practiced for many years, perhaps for a lifetime. To many, perhaps most, of those who practice them, they do not disclose themselves as vices at all during life.

Virtues, on the other hand, often appear so harsh and rugged, they require the sacrifice of so much present happiness, at least, and the results, which alone prove them to be virtues, are often so distant and obscure, in fact, so absolutely invisible to the minds of many, especially of the young, that, from the very nature of things, there can be no universal, or even general, knowledge that they are virtues. In truth, the studies of profound philosophers have been expended — if not wholly in vain, certainly with very small results — in efforts to draw the lines between the virtues and the vices.

If, then, it became so difficult, so nearly impossible, in most cases, to determine what is, and what is not, vice — and especially if it be so difficult, in nearly all cases, to determine where virtue ends, and vice begins — and if these questions, which no one can really and truly determine for anybody but himself, are not to be left free and open for experiment by all, each person is deprived of the highest of all his rights as a human being, to wit, his right to inquire,

investigate, reason, try experiments, judge, and
ascertain for himself what is, to him, virtue, and
what is, to him, vice — in other words: what, on
the whole, conduces to his happiness, and what, on
the whole, tends to his unhappiness. If this great
right is not to be left free and open to all, then each
man's whole right, as a reasoning human being, to
"liberty and the pursuit of happiness," is denied
him."

If we can sit back and honestly assess what are considered vices versus virtues, then we come to the realization that it is not an issue of trespass so much as the determination being one of consciousness. The *ideas* offend more than one being trespassed upon by the specific behavior. Within the herd structure of compliance, it is the consciousness that revolts at ideas that counter that of the individual, the person doesn't like the *idea* that someone may be doing something they find personally objectionable to their own way of thinking. When we look at the fact that what is determined to be acceptable has been passed down from on high, from some authority figure or another (including some God), through unwavering traditions of sameness and fear of going against the herd, then, as Spooner notes, the line between vice and virtue blurs into absolute obscurity and arguably becomes perceptual nonsense.

To become a free consciousness, one must weigh everything they think they know by the measure of whether their presumed knowledge is based on experience, or simply on the say-so of others. In virtually all cases the individual seeking cognitive freedom is going to discover that what they think and believe is not based on experience, but is a result of second-hand information handed down by others and enforced by their herds because everyone *believes* it to be true. This is conventional wisdom, not true wisdom.

7. Humanity is at a Crossroad

Humanity presently stands at a crossroad of difficult choices. Once more our species is faced with the strong possibility of another global war which is liable to be more devastating than the last two World Wars, given the destructive potential of the present weapons arsenals available. Contrary to conventional wisdom, both of the last World Wars were manipulated into taking place by the Fabian elite and their allies in the financial system. There is more than enough documentation to substantiate this claim, and the words of the Fabian globalist controllers have never hesitated to state their designs, although their words are not reported to the public at large. For more comprehensive information on this subject, the person seeking wisdom would do well to invest the time to read *Fabian Freeway: High Road to Socialism in the USA,* written by Rose L. Martin in 1966. Another informative read on this information can be found with Carroll Quigley's book, *The Anglo-American Establishment.* Both of these informative volumes can be found in free .pdf downloads on the internet. A much harder to find and more recent volume on this subject is *The Milner-Fabian Conspiracy* by Ioan Ratui. Although Ratui's book was published in 2012, it is already out of print except through one seller I found on Amazon out of the UK.

While the current media circus in the U.S. is distracting its citizens with allegations about Russian collusion with Donald Trump, it is the Fabian Anglo-American Establishment that is behind all the present turmoil in the U.S. political arena. With people like Hillary Clinton and an army of Democrat liberals working in collusion with the Fabian George Soros, Americans are being sold just one more cognitive illusion which may well lead to a real civil war in the U.S. This is the manner in which public perception is manipulated on all sides to destroy nations using Marxist revolutionary ideologies and Fabian principles of gradualism using propaganda and mass psychology as their primary weapons. It has taken the Fabian brainwashing machine generations to bring the U.S. to this point of potential self-destruction as a free nation, and their agenda has been frighteningly successful. What is of even more concern is how utterly clueless people are about the cognitive manipulation that has taken place to lead humanity to this point in its lack of cognitive evolution.

In Europe, the issue of national sovereignty is challenged by an influx of Muslims who will, in little time, eventually outbreed the Europeans and make all of Europe nothing more than an extended territory of Islam. Anyone who protests this national destruction by an invasion of hostile refugees is pilloried in the press and shouted down by media pundits and politicians who are all in the pockets of the Fabian elite money powers. Whether the reader wants to accept this reality or not, the Fabians themselves have left more than enough documentation on their hidden agenda to be irrefutable. Denial will not alter this truth, and such denial is quickly leading to a world in which humanity will find utter chaos and finally a global totalitarian state controlled by these elite and their lackeys. This is not conspiracy theory, this is conspiracy fact, and humanity refuses to accept this fact because its upsets its perceptual worldview.

As comprehensive an investigation as the aforementioned works present, they all missed the element of the spiritual side of this globalist equation, paying more attention to the political and financial aspects and completely overlooking the massive influence of the Theosophical Society in collusion with the Fabians and secret societies like the Freemasons and the Jesuit Order in the Catholic Church. When the Fabians took over Theosophy they split their ranks, with the Fabian Alice Bailey setting up headquarters in the U.S. and the Fabian Annie Besant setting up headquarters in India.

Indian religion was a hodge-podge collection of many different forms of worshipping gods and goddesses. It was the Fabian Theosophist Sri Aurobindo who coined the term Hinduism to identify all these disparate traditions under one homogenous banner. The word Hindu itself is ancient, but it referred to the region known as India (Indus Valley region), not as a homogenous religious designation. The Theosophists started folding world religions under their homogenizing banner in India under the direction of Annie Besant, Sri Aurobindo and other Fabian Theosophist activists. The Indian independence movement against Great Britain was spearheaded by the Fabian, Theosophy-trained Mahatma Gandhi.

In the U.S., we see the move toward the homogenization of religions starting when Alice Bailey and her cohorts collaborated in rewriting their own versions of Christianity, mixed with Masonic-influenced religions like Christian Science. Eventually, political Zionism entered the scene being preached from the pulpits to Protestant believers to support the Fabian idea about forming the Zionist State of Israel. With a blending of inorganic hive teachings by alleged Ascended Masters, this Theosophical homogenization served as the foundation for the modern New Age movement, with people like the Fabian Aldous Huxley pushing the usage of hallucinogenic drugs to attain enlightenment in collusion with Timothy Leary and the Esalen Institute in Big Sur, California in the 1960's, which was admittedly ground zero for launching the New Age movement.

The *modus operandi* of the Lucis Trust organization created by Alice Bailey is the same as that of the Fabian Society. Both mask their actions hiding behind tens of thousands of 'charitable trusts', think-tanks and other tax free organizations worldwide, keeping their actions hidden behind these organizations and far removed from the eyes of the public. They play a cognitive shell game of deception, hiding behind the agenda of promoting feel-good doctrines promoting humanitarianism, compassion and world peace, but the only peace they seek is that of a Marxist totalitarian global tyranny with them sitting atop a hierarchal pyramid of bureaucracies and controlled corporate and government stooges. The consciousness of the average person is nothing but malleable clay in their hands, and the public only makes its decisions based on superficial perceptions of difference, which in actuality, do not exist beyond propagandized rhetorical opposition.

The Fabian Society has infiltrated all political parties and they control both the left and the right, insuring that no matter where the public looks for answers, Fabian propaganda feeds their individual desires where the individual only thinks there is a difference between political parties and ideologies. This is how the management of superficial perceptions keeps all of humanity bound in a system of cognitive tyranny, and the vast majority of people cannot see beyond these superficial perceptions to perceive the truth behind the illusion. Being swayed by their emotions and their 'beliefs', humanity is easy to prod into the cognitive corrals designed by the Fabian elite through fear and propaganda. The world is an illusion, but not the physical world. The illusion is a cognitive illusion of perception. It is no different than the sleight of hand used by magicians throughout the ages, except that the consciousness of all humanity is at stake in this global perceptual illusion.

As an individual that is interested in your own cognitive freedom, you have to see through this illusion or you will simply remain an emotionally-reactive pawn to this game of cognitive deception. The global mind controllers know exactly how to push your emotional buttons and you allow it through your own fears and anxieties. These are the people that refined psychology and turned it into a weapon of cognitive control. They wrote the books on the subject and they are fully adept in using these tools against all of humanity. For humanity to advance and evolve into a more responsible and mature species, this type of cognitive manipulation must be recognized and transcended. This is true wisdom.

No one can make any kind of informed decision on anything without the valid information on which to base that decision. Propaganda and populism are not valid information, they are the tools used by those who manipulate entire cultures through superficial presentations of data to excite the emotions of their selected audience. Until one can transcend such emotional reactivity in themselves, they will ever be a slave to such manipulations of their consciousness. It is the ego itself that is driven by the fears and anxieties that plague the human species. It is the ego's own sense of personal arrogance that creates the platform for denying the truth so it can embrace comfortable lies. Only one who can transcend the hapiym-infected ego within themselves is the one who will gain true wisdom and not simplistic philosophical speculations about wisdom. True wisdom comes when one can face the truth unabashedly and without fear of what that truth presents. To do otherwise only leaves one a prisoner to a system of cognitive awareness that keeps them ever enslaved to the ideas of others, always reacting to outside influences, and fearful of anything that challenges there programmed beliefs.

It is the journey inward to assess our own beliefs and shortcomings where we find the resolution to all of the external manipulation we have each been subjected to throughout or lives by our parents, our teachers, our peers, our traditions and our cultures. When we take this sincere journey within ourselves, and honestly analyze why we believe what we believe, we find that the great majority of these beliefs came about because someone else told us we should believe it, and very often, there is little genuine personal experience to substantiate such beliefs. Our beliefs are the stuff of illusion, and upon scrutiny, they fail to support themselves, regardless of conventional wisdom or herd consensus agreement on such matters. Spooner observed it this way:

> *"In the midst of this endless variety of opinion, what man, or what body of men, has the right to say, in regard to any particular action, or course of action, "We have tried this experiment, and determined every question involved in it. We have determined it, not only for ourselves, but for all others. And, as to all those who are weaker than we, we will coerce them to act in obedience to our conclusion. We will suffer no further experiment or inquiry by any one, and, consequently, no further acquisition of knowledge by anybody"?*
>
> *Who are the men who have the right to say this? Certainly there are none such. The men who really do say it are either shameless impostors and tyrants, who would stop the progress of knowledge, and usurp absolute control over the minds and bodies of their fellow men — and are therefore to be resisted instantly, and to the last extent — or they are themselves too ignorant of their own weaknesses, and of their true relations to other*

men, to be entitled to any other consideration than sheer pity or contempt.

"It is a natural impossibility that a government should have a right to punish men for their vices; because it is impossible that a government should have any rights except such as the individuals composing it had previously had as individuals."

We know, however, that there are such men as these in the world. Some of them attempt to exercise their power only within a small sphere, to wit, upon their children, their neighbors, their townsmen, and their countrymen. Others attempt to exercise it on a larger scale.

For example, an old man at Rome, aided by a few subordinates, attempts to decide all questions of virtue and vice — that is, of truth or falsehood, especially in matters of religion. He claims to know and teach what religious ideas and practices are conducive, or fatal, to a man's happiness, not only in this world, but in that which is to come. He claims to be miraculously inspired for the performance of this work — thus virtually acknowledging, like a sensible man, that nothing short of miraculous inspiration would qualify him for it.

This miraculous inspiration, however, has been ineffectual to enable him to settle more than a very few questions. The most important to which common mortals can attain is an implicit belief in his (the pope's) infallibility! and, secondly, that the blackest vices of which they can be guilty are to believe and declare that he is only a man like the rest of them!

It required some 1500 or 1800 years to enable him to reach definite conclusions on these two vital points. Yet it would seem that the first of these must necessarily be preliminary to his settlement of any other questions; because, until his own infallibility is determined, he can authoritatively decide nothing else.

He has, however, heretofore attempted or pretended to settle a few others. And he may, perhaps, attempt or pretend to settle a few more in the future, if he shall continue to find anybody to listen to him. But his success, thus far, certainly does not encourage the belief that he will be able to settle all questions of virtue and vice, even in his peculiar department of religion, in time to meet the necessities of mankind.

He, or his successors, will undoubtedly be compelled, at no distant day, to acknowledge that he has undertaken a task to which all his miraculous inspiration was inadequate; and that, of necessity, each human being must be left to settle all questions of this kind for himself. And it is not unreasonable to expect that all other popes, in other and lesser spheres, will some time have cause to come to the same conclusion.

No one, certainly, not claiming supernatural inspiration, should undertake a task to which obviously nothing less than such inspiration is adequate. And, clearly, no one should surrender his own judgment to the teachings of others, unless he be first convinced that these others have something more than ordinary human knowledge on this subject.

If those persons, who fancy themselves gifted with both the power and the right to define and punish other men's vices, would but turn their thoughts inwardly, they would probably find that they have a great work to do at home — and that, when that shall have been completed, they will be little disposed to do more toward correcting the vices of others than simply to give to others the results of their experience and observation. In this sphere their labors may possibly be useful; but, in the sphere of infallibility and coercion, they will probably, for well-known reasons, meet with even less success in the future than such men have met with in the past."

Again, these are wise words and valid observations, and it is from such questioning that every individual must launch their own quest for discovery of their own conscious advancement. As a species, we can no longer rely on our accepted authorities to dictate to us what our perception of reality should be according to their own limited human dictates. As Spooner asked, *"Who are these men who have the right to say this?"* The global elite have appointed themselves as judge, jury and executioner to all who disagree with their mandates. The academics, popes, imams, politicians and the self-appointed dictators of human consciousness are all merely men with first cognition over-inflated egos who feel they are the chosen ones to manipulate the rest of humanity. Your neighbors, friends, coworkers, family, and even you the reader are merely parrots to these diverse and varied opinions rendered by these presumed authorities throughout the ages. Their thoughts are your thoughts, and each human is blissfully unaware of this cognitive chicanery. Every ego will defend its own opinions to justify its own self-image, yet this self-image is itself an illusion, a simulacrum of what a human can truly be. You are merely just another cog in a cognitive infernal machine, yet you alone have the power to change it . . . if you will.

8. The Silver Lining

Despite what may seem like a grim presentation, there is a silver lining to this story of humanity finding true wisdom as a species, and that is the dormant potential in the human race to transcend all of this cognitive tyranny. There have been enough forerunners to this process to stand as evidence that this can be achieved with the right information and the diligence of the individual to face the truth and transcend the world of perceptual illusions we think is our collective reality. One who chooses to live in the world of lies will die in that same world of illusion, never knowing what it means to be a cognitively aware, fully functional and truly wise human being. This has been the human legacy since we were created as a species, and it is past time we change this revolving door of repeating historical errors and lack of cognitive advancement. If we don't, we are very likely to make ourselves extinct based on our own collective mental neurosis at the hands of the hapiym mind virus, becoming just another failed experiment in the evolutionary cycle of the universe.

Like Nietzsche, Jesus, Buddha and don Juan, I have crossed the threshold into the second cognition level of awareness, and I can fully understand the vision they tried to share with this world. This is not personal braggadocio, nor is it blustering ego arrogance. It is simply a fact that the reader is left to determine on their own. This cognitive reality is within your reach provided you are willing to do the work required to claim your own cognitive sovereignty, despite the hands of the herd continually grasping at you to drag you back down into their illusionary reality. To achieve this is a monumental task, but the reward is worth the perilous journey to remove yourself from the corrals of herd conformity. It all comes down to making a choice, and each individual is now faced with a choice as to which version of reality they wish to embrace. One version is well worn and comfortable and leads to perpetual dead ends of repeating errors. The second cognition version leads to unlimited potential in advancing humanity as a species as well as continual cognitive advancement.

Each of these teachers used their own methods to try and awaken a humanity lost, living in a world of perceptual illusion. All of their teachings were either corrupted or misunderstood by people operating from a cognitive system that cannot see beyond its own limitations. With our teachings, humanity is once again given information that can alter its world for the better and set a new course for human cognitive advancement. As with these other teachers, the question must be asked, who has the ears to hear these words and act upon them? Do you?

All one has to do is take a look at the situation in the world today to see that humanity has taken a wrong turn where its destiny as a species is concerned. We can either take the offramp to destruction, as we have done time and again throughout recorded history, or we can gain wisdom as a species and take a different course; a course of our choosing and not the choosing of self-appointed authorities whose only goal is to keep all of humanity enslaved to their crass ego desires for power and the accumulation of all the wealth on the planet. There is an adage that says knowledge is power, but I'm here to tell you that wisdom is more powerful than knowledge alone. Knowledge has led humanity to this crossroad and has shown itself to be patently insufficient to guide our species when it is wisdom that is needed to change the course of human history for the better. If we don't develop true wisdom as a species and stop denying the truth in favor of perceptual lies, then all the knowledge in the world is nothing but useless intellectual masturbation. Knowledge without the wisdom to apply it is useless, if not downright dangerous.

As a species, we must stop relying on the belief in otherworldly intervention to save us from ourselves. The invisible gods of religious manufacture, the fictitious makers of the universe, do not and never have existed. They are just another perceptual illusion to keep humanity's eyes focused on a fictional hereafter and not on correcting itself as a species. God is going to fix it, yet there is not one verifiable scrap of evidence that these fictional, all-powerful gods have ever intervened in the affairs of man on this planet. It is simply a vaporous belief, as tangible as trying to catch fog, yet almost 2/3 of humanity continues to believe and rely on this fantasy relinquishment of personal responsibility with their eyes ever focused on a hereafter that was nothing but the residence of the hapiym hive virus. Don't worry about how shitty conditions are in this life, let God fix it in the next one. How much more irresponsible can an individual become than to give up their lives to a fictional belief in an unproven 'afterlife'? Do not take down the tyrants, they work for the Devil,

God's going to fix it all in the end! So, do nothing in this life to make yourself better, simply believe and pray to your gods, and above all *obey!*

This is humanity's curse; the obedience syndrome. The reliance on authority is so ingrained in this species that it is the rare individual indeed who can rise above this cognitive programming of perpetual dependence on others to make their decisions for them. This is the challenge it takes to become a person of wisdom, to question all authority and ask why one should remain obedient to it. What makes an 'authority' an authority? A piece of paper handed down by a school? An alleged communication with some God or angels? Being born into a wealthy family? The right royal bloodline? These are questions that every person should ask themselves before bending their knee to any authority figure. The only authority I lay claim to is my own experience and the observed experiences of others who have achieved what I have through similar processes. I don't ask the reader to take my word for it, but invite you to experience it for yourself, for with that experience you will gain both knowledge and wisdom. This is the only way to advance your own consciousness and to become your own authority. To do less only leaves you a slave to the ideas of others, bending your knee at their altars of authority.

With the exception of Friedrich Nietzsche, the wisdom teachers throughout time were not college educated. For the most part they started out as average men, with the possible exception of the Buddha, which should tell you that it is not intellectualism that leads one to wisdom. All the college degrees in the world have not taught a single intellectual academic in the world the wisdom required to advance human consciousness. The intellectual classes philosophize and speculate what they perceive to be wisdom, but at the end of the day, throughout history, they have not provided a single cogent answer to this question about how one becomes wise. Spooner observed this and I offer the same observation for the simple reason; it happens to be correct.

You have it in you to achieve this, provided you have the guts and stamina to go against your herd programming and transcend the effects of the hapiym virus embedded in your psyche. If I can do this, so can you. You don't have to get out in public and wave banners and shout slogans to accomplish this. You are not here to 'save the world' any more than I am. The only person anyone has control over is themselves, and it is few indeed that choose to exercise that control to grow themselves beyond the constraints of their cultural programming. You are not going to evolve your consciousness railing against the first cognition machine. You are not going to change that system from within, so thinking that you are obligated to 'save' others who choose to remain living the illusion will only bring you heartbreak and discouragement. This is a personal journey on which only you can embark and come out the other side as a stronger, more cognitively evolved human being.

Everything in the first cognition system of consciousness is based on collectivism. It is a mentality spawned by the hapiym virus itself with its inherent nature to cluster in hives. Every human has been infected with this collectivist hive/herding mentality without exception. Your mission is to transcend the effects of this virus within yourself. You can't do anything for any other person unless they make the same choice you do to heal yourself from the effects of this mental infection. The fact that this herding instinct of the virus is embedded in your own mind will make your journey a difficult one indeed, since this programming will always turn you to the herd for validation and solidarity with your own individual herds. You will not find validation for your efforts in the first cognition, only scorn and ridicule from those whose consciousness remains infected by the effects of the virus. It is a lonely journey that most fail to complete because of the pressure induced by their friends and loved ones to return to the state of *normalcy* mandated by the herd mentality. The herd functions on compliance, not resistance to its mandates, and anyone who chooses to grow beyond these constraints is an automatic target for criticism and brow-beating to bring one back into the fold. This is the rule, not the exception to this process.

To trod this road is a cognitively painful endeavor for everyone, especially when we realize that not only have we bought the lies of the illusion for so long, but that we have been lying to ourselves to embrace the ideas of the herd. This is the greatest hurdle to transcending the effects of the virus, for we each have to admit that even what we believed to be ourselves under the effects of the hapiym infection are a total fabrication. This realization leads to a sense of nihilism, which is defined as *"the rejection of all religious and moral principles, often in the belief that life is meaningless."* When we are ultimately confronted with and accept the truth about the world we live in being a perceptual illusion, a sense of cognitive defeatism kicks in and we feel that there is no purpose in moving forward, for everything we found value in becomes meaningless in the face of truth.

In regard to this phase of nihilistic defeatism, Friedrich Nietzsche wrote in *The Will to Power:*

*"Nihilism as a psychological state will have to be reached, **first,** when we have sought a "meaning" in all events that is not there: so the seeker eventually becomes discouraged. Nihilism, then, is the recognition of the long **waste** of* strength, the agony of the "in vain," insecurity, the lack of any opportunity to recover and to regain composure - being ashamed in front of oneself, as if one had ***deceived*** *oneself all too long. - This meaning could have been: the "fulfillment" of some highest ethical canon in all events, the moral world order; or the growth of love and harmony in the intercourse of beings; or the gradual approximation of a state of universal happiness; or even the development toward a state of universal annihilation - any goal at least constitutes some meaning. What all these notions have in common is that something is to be **achieved** through the process - and now one realizes that becoming aims at nothing and achieves **nothing.** - Thus, disappointment regarding an alleged aim of becoming as a cause of nihilism: whether regarding a specific aim or, universalized, the*

realization that all previous hypotheses about aims that concern the whole "evolution" are inadequate (man no longer the collaborator, let alone the center, of becoming).

*Nihilism as a psychological state is reached, **secondly,** when one has posited a totality, a systematization, indeed any organization in all events, and underneath all events, and a soul that longs to admire and revere has wallowed in the idea of some supreme form of domination and administration (-if the soul be that of a logician, complete consistency and real dialectic are quite sufficient to reconcile it to everything). Some sort of unity, some form of "monism": this faith suffices to give man a deep feeling of standing in the context of, and being dependent on, some whole that is infinitely superior to him, and he sees himself as a mode of the deity. - "The well-being of the universal demands the devotion of the individual" - but behold, there is no such universal! At bottom, man has lost the faith in his own value when no infinitely valuable whole works through him; i.e., he conceived such a whole in order **to be able to believe in his own value.***

*Nihilism as psychological state has yet a **third** and **last** form. Given these two insights, that becoming has no goal and that underneath all becoming there is no grand unity in which the* *individual could immerse himself completely as in an element of supreme value, an escape remains: to pass sentence on this whole world of becoming as a deception and to invent a world beyond it, a true world. But as soon as man finds out how that world is fabricated solely from psychological needs, and how he has absolutely no right to it, the last form of nihilism comes into being: it includes disbelief in any metaphysical world and forbids itself any belief in a **true** world. Having reached this standpoint, one grants the reality of becoming as the only reality, forbids oneself every kind of clandestine access to afterworlds and false divinities - but **cannot endure this world though one does not want to deny it.***

*What has happened, at bottom? The feeling of valuelessness was reached with the realization that the overall character of existence may not be interpreted by means of the concept of "aim," the concept of "unity," or the concept of "truth." Existence has no goal or end; any comprehensive unity in the plurality of events is lacking: the character of existence is not "true," is false. One simply lacks any reason for convincing oneself that there is a true world. Briefly: the categories "aim," "unity," "being" which we used to project some value into the world - we **pull out** again; so the world looks **valueless.***"

I wrote about this stage of cognitive transition in my book *Demystifying the Mystical*, although I did not use the word nihilism to describe the feeling of 'what's the use' in continuing with this process when we finally come face to face with the fact that our entire life has been based on second-hand storytelling and illusions created by others. What Nietzsche capably describes in the foregoing passages are the transition through the dark night of the soul when one finally has to confront the truth they have denied all their lives, while embracing and living the perceptual illusion of the first cognition version of reality.

This is the point at which the ego and the hapiym virus is on its knees waiting for the final knock-out punch before the real you can step into its own power and claim its birthright as an autonomous human being, relying on no God or authority, nor even the herd, to define you. This phase of nihilistic thinking is where many people on the road to the second cognition fail and cave into defeatism and the last bastion of the hapiym virus - *self-pity* over the loss of it all. If one gives into this woeful self-pity, then the hapiym virus wins and you will never advance into the second cognition to achieve your transcendence beyond the perceptual illusion. You will simple remain just another hapless victim to the hapiym virus infection and will die a hopeless and broken person, unable to live in either the first cognition world or move forward into the second cognition because you have embraced victimhood. You will not find your own value if you remain caught in this no man's land of nihilistic defeatism and self-pity. Only one who has crossed this dark abyss and come out the other side a whole, fully functional human being can understand what Nietzsche is relating in these passages. To anyone who has not passed through these gates of hell, it is only difficult to understand philosophy.

The wise individual that pulls through this dark passageway to the realm of second cognition awareness is then able to see the valuelessness of all the rules, regulations, authorities, traditions and morals in a world dictated by others to keep one dependent on that system of herd ideologies. At this stage, the individual must truly stand alone and apart from the herd, and as Nietzsche termed it, a revaluation of all morals becomes a mandate where the individual must set their own guidelines of behavior. This does not amount to the concept put forth by Aleister Crowley in is esoteric teachings, *"Do as thou wilt"*, for his teachings also include the concept of manipulating others through magic. To do so is to perform trespass on others, and the wise sage is above such acts of trespass.

The first and primary rule in this revaluation of morals is that one does not trespass on others. Once one accepts the responsibility to not trespass on another's person, property or their consciousness, then one's individual rules become their own. The responsible and cognitively mature human being sets their own values and standards to live by without some authority, God, or herd mandating what is right for them as a free individual. As Spooner noted, one man's vice is another's virtue. When you become the author of your own life, such authoritative rules to govern the herds of the cognitively enslaved are no longer your concern.

When one operates strictly from the standpoint of a paranoid and hapiym-infected ego personality, they can scarcely comprehend how a second cognition human being can comport themselves without fear and rules to guide them. It goes beyond the comprehension level of first cognition reality to imagine a fully responsible individual with the composure to manage their own affairs without some authority to tell them what to do. The first cognition world of illusion is filled with suspicion and distrust, and one lost in that cognitive quagmire can't understand a humanity not enslaved by such fears, yet that is exactly with this book and all our others works are inviting humanity to learn. Contrary to popular propaganda, this will not result in chaos, but will result in a civility never before experienced by a humanity that has always been ruled over by authorities and their laws; ever obedient and subservient to such authority.

What you are invited to learn from this book is the wisdom sought after for generations of humanity, but which has always been out of reach under the authoritative systems of control. As Nietzsche noted, we have to have a system of new values to suit a species with a mature consciousness, but until humanity itself decides to stop its fruitless efforts living in a reality of lies and illusions, the first cognition false reality will continue until it reaches its final conclusion. At the present time, the outlook for this reality and this species looks pretty grim. It is possible that after enough bloodshed and horror has taken place that this species might actually choose to wake up in mass and decide to change itself, but until such a thing occurs, it is up to the individuals who will be the forerunners of the willful evolutionary change to do it for themselves.

The next level of human advancement will only arrive with a more advanced form of human consciousness, and that is not to be found through the Transhumanist agenda of blending human and animal genetics, nor though turning the human race into cyborgs by merging our consciousness with machines we created. These types of artificial innovation are what the Fabian elite call human evolution, for they are convinced, in their own sublime arrogance, that humanity can't redeem itself. It must be controlled by these self-appointed rulers who decide who lives and who dies and under what condition the human race shall be managed by them. This is the present reality in which you live, like it or not. You have a choice to continue to be a slave to this system, or you can choose to grow wisdom and transcend it into Nietzsche's 'mountain air' of cognitive freedom. The door to the second cognition stands waiting. Shall we expect your arrival?

References

Author's referenced books

Willful Evolution

We Are Not Alone – Part 3: The Luciferian Agenda of the Mother Goddess

The Evolution of Consciousness Series

The Energetic War Against Humanity: The 6,000 Year War Against Hunan Cognitive Advancement

Demystifying the Mystical

External References

The Island of Dr. Moreau – H.G. Wells

Shrinking the Technosphere – Dmitri Orlov

The Psychology of Socialism – Gustave Le Bon

The Will to Power – Friedrich Nietzsche

Thus Spoke Zarathustra – Friedrich Nietzsche

Beyond Good and Evil – Friedrich Nietzsche

Instincts of the Herd in Peace and War – Wilfred Trotter

The Psychology of Suggestion – Boris Sidis

Ecce Homo – Friedrich Nietzsche

Vices are not Crimes – Lysander Spooner

Fabian Freeway: High Road to Socialism in the USA – Rose Martin

The Anglo-American Establishment – Carroll Quigley

The Evolution of Consciousness Series

Book 1

A Philosophy for the Average Man: An Uncommon Solution to a World Without Common Sense by Endall Beall

Book 2

Willful Evolution: The Path to Advanced Cognitive Awareness and a Personal Shift in Consciousness by Endall Beall

Book 3

Demystifying the Mystical: Exposing Myths of the Mystical and the Supernatural by Providing Solutions to the Spirit Path and Human Evolution by Endall Beall

Book 4

Navigating into the Second Cognition: The Map for your journey into higher Conscious Awareness by Endall Beall

Book 5

The Energy Experience: Energy work for the Second Cognition by Mrs. Endall Beall

Book 6

We Are Not Alone – Part 1: Advancing Cognitive Awareness in an Interactive Universe by Endall Beall

Book 7

We Are Not Alone – Part 2: Advancing Cognitive Awareness through Historical Revelations - Endall Beall

Book 8

Advanced Teachings for the Second Cognition by Mrs. Endall Beall

Book 9

We Are Not Alone – Part 3: The Luciferian Agenda of the Mother Goddess by Endall Beall

Companion Volumes to The Evolution of Consciousness Series

False Prophecies, Reassessing Buddha and the Call to the Second Cognition by Endall Beall

Operator's Manual for the True Spirit Warrior by Endall Beall

Spiritual Pragmatism: A Practical Approach to Spirit Work in a World Controlled by Ego by Endall Beall

Revamping Psychology: A Critique of Transpersonal Psychology Viewed From the Second Cognition by Endall Beall & Mrs. Endall Beall

Second Cognition Series

Book 1

The New Paradigm Transcripts: Teachings for a New Tomorrow by Endall Beall & Doug Michael

Book 2

Breaking the Chains of the First Cognition: Tools for Understanding the Path to the Second Cognition by Endall Beall & Doug Michael

Book 3

PSOYCA – Road to the Second Cognition by Endall Beall & Doug Michael

Book 4

The Energetic War Against Humanity: The 6,000 Year War Against Human Cognitive Advancement by Endall Beall

In Progress –

Book 5

The Cognitive Illusion of History: How Humanity Has Been Controlled Through Selective and Biased Historical Reporting by Endall Beall & Doug Michael

Book 6

The Second Cognition Toolbox: Requirements for Advancing Your Consciousness by Endall Beall

Book 7

No Trespassing: Creating a New World Based on Mutual Respect by Endall Beall

Companion Volumes to the Second Cognition Series

Understanding Wisdom: A Treatise on Wisdom Viewed from the Second Cognition by Endall Beall

For questions or inquiries contact the authors at Demystifyingthemystical.com